BEYOND THE BABYLIFT

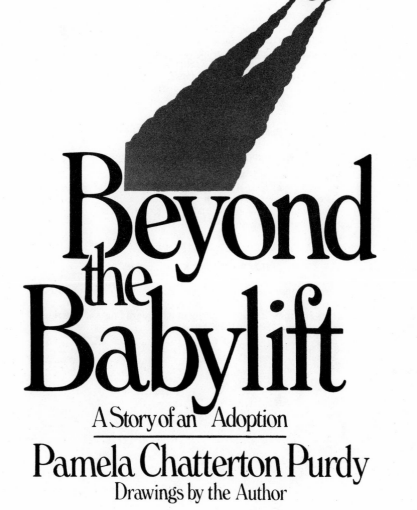

Beyond the Babylift

A Story of an Adoption

Pamela Chatterton Purdy

Drawings by the Author

ABINGDON PRESS

Nashville

BEYOND THE BABYLIFT: A STORY OF AN ADOPTION

This book is printed on acid-free paper.

Library of Congress Cataloging-in-Publication Data

PURDY, PAMELA CHATTERTON, 1940–
    Beyond the babylift.   1. Adoption—United States—Case studies.
    2. Intercountry adoption—United States—Case studies.
    3. Interracial adoption—United States—Case studies.
    4. Purdy, Pamela Chatterton, 1940 – —Diaries.
    I. Title
HV875.55.P87   1987   362.7'34'0924 [B]   87-11532

ISBN 0-687-03082-X (alk. paper)

Scripture quotations noted KJV are from King James Version of the Bible.

All others are from The New Testament in Modern English, copyright ©
J. B. Phillips 1958, 1959, 1960, 1972.

MANUFACTURED BY THE PARTHENON PRESS AT
NASHVILLE, TENNESSEE, UNITED STATES OF AMERICA

To my husband, David

*The book itself speaks to his
constant love and caring.*

———————————————

BEYOND THE BABYLIFT

CONTENTS

INTRODUCTION

W hy adopt nonwhite children? David and I would respond, Why not?

We were married in June 1963. David had just graduated from Yale Divinity School; I had just graduated from the University of New Hampshire as an art major. That first summer, Martin Luther King led his march on Washington.

David's first ministerial appointment catapulted us from campus life to a black section of Chicago. The Ecumenical Institute was our first home, and *Ebony* magazine was the site of my first job.

The civil rights movement was questioning the church's viability! Did we really love our neighbor? Did we believe in community? Frightening as it was for some, Martin Luther King was challenging both the churched and the unchurched to walk on the water! The Word had flesh once again! My sweet Sunday school theology was exploding with new meaning. The church was becoming part of a dynamic Spirit movement for change. And David and I were deeply committed to that change.

Suddenly I was seeing Scripture in a new light! In a magazine, a full-page advertisement portrayed a white mother holding a black child. The parents of the mother, posing for this family photo, had very worried expressions. The caption read, "You always said you wanted grandchildren."

The flesh-and-blood Spirit movement was taking on new forms all around us. Had Christ been raised from the dead only to never walk among us again? "I am not a ghost" echoed in my mind. I knew it was from Scripture. I looked it up and found it in Luke 24:38. On the road to Emmaus, it was as if Jesus were speaking to those grandparents, and to all of us.

"Why are you so worried?" he asked, "and why do doubts arise in your minds? Look at my hands and my feet—it is really I myself! Feel me and see; ghosts have no flesh or bones as you see that I have" (vss. 38-40).

It all seemed so clear and simple. The freedom from fear was exhilarating! Hence it was with a certain naiveté that David and I began our journey together.

My employment in *Ebony's* art department began in September, and on November 22, President Kennedy was shot! Phones rang with the tragic news. The hum in those busy offices stopped. Stunned and crying, we rushed to the large TV in the lobby. Grief, rage, and anger creased face after face!

"God-damn nigger-haters," said one.

"The President should have known he was a dead man when he allowed that march!" said another.

Television images from Dallas were blurred by my tears. Paralyzed, I called David at the Institute. Yes, he had heard. Not only had he heard, but he—like the rest of us—was seeing again and again the scene in Dallas, the roses, Jackie and her blood-stained suit.

Later that day in the company break room, several of us sat in silence.

"Blood gonna flow in the streets," muttered Carla.

She was staring right at me. A slight young woman, she could not have weighed more than ninety pounds.

"What do you mean?" I asked. I turned to Sarah, another co-worker. "What's she talking about, Sarah?"

Sarah worked in the photo lab next to the art department. She was the mother of two boys. We often talked and had become quite close.

"What's she talking about? I'll tell you what Carla is talking about! Do you remember the day I had you call a realtor and get me and my husband an appointment to see a house? Your white voice went just so far, honey. Soon as that man saw the color of our skin, it was, 'So sorry, that house has just been sold!' That ain't the first time I've run into hate. I've been putting up with white man's shit all my life! One day blacks gonna have enough! One day someone is gonna shoot a white person! Then another! Then two or three of us blacks gonna join in! Pretty soon the gutter gonna run red."

"Sarah! That's not what Dr. King would want!"

"Not what Dr. King would want?" A small smile crept across her face. "We don't *all* agree with Dr. King, you know! Malcolm X is the only one who can help us now."

"Sarah, don't you know how much hatred Malcolm has for *all* whites? How can killing in the streets help anything? I'm white. Am I the devil?"

An eerie silence hung about me.

"Sarah, what if *I* were on that street when shooting broke out?"

Sarah looked me straight in the eye. "Honey, you'd be a dead woman. I'd pull the trigger on you, just like on any other white." She got up and left the room.

That was the first time I encountered black rage at *Ebony*—the first of many times! I had run smack into the injustices of the white world. In light of that rage, I was discovering myself to be a white liberal idealist. How simple I thought change could be.

David and I adopted Ronald, our first black son, in 1971. Kristen had been born in 1966 and Jessica in 1969. When Jessica was age one and a half, we went to the adoption agency to request a son. We knew the only available children would be nonwhite.

Beyond the Babylift begins with the arrival of our second son, Hoāng. Of black and Vietnamese heritage, he was flown to this country during the babylift in 1975. It was then that a friend encouraged me to keep a diary. I will always be grateful that I did—it has become a journal of reflection time and again. As any parent knows, raising children can be difficult. Add the special dimensions of adoption, differing ethnic background and race, and it can be even more difficult.

Periodically, I find it therapeutic to reread earlier entries. It helps me to keep perspective when times get tough. Sometimes I laugh; sometimes I cry. This book is an attempt to put flesh on our struggle to be a family!

DECISION

Thursday, May 15, 1975

The babylift from Vietnam had been in full swing for about a month, and every day thousands of children were being flown to all parts of the country. Couples with active, approved applications for U.S. adoptions were telephoned by Friends of Children of Vietnam to ask whether they would consider a Vietnamese child. Our call came on Thursday, May 15.

"Yes, we'd consider a Vietnamese child, but only if he were half black." David and I had been hoping to adopt another black son because our experience with Ronald, then almost 7, had been so joyful. Kristen, then 8, and Jessica, 5, our biological daughters, had truly accepted him as their brother.

My husand, David, is a United Methodist minister. During the turbulent sixties we had been very socially active. In an emotional time of split churches and divided family feelings, we at least had "put our money where our mouth was," according to my father-in-law.

But the climate of adoption had changed since Ronald's placement in 1971. Because of increased black consciousness, social workers were insisting that black children be adopted only by black families. While we sympathized with the need for a black identity, we believed that a loving home was of primary importance. Children of mixed parentage also were denied to us, even though we saw ourselves as a racially mixed family.

Yes, they had a five-year-old half-black, half-Vietnamese child. His name was Hoāng. Would we consider him? If so, could we fly to Denver tomorrow to pick him up? The question took us by surprise. Why the rush? The social worker gave the reason for the urgent placement. The facility in which the children were housed was a new nursing home, scheduled to open on Monday. Those children had to be out! Of 450 children, Hoāng was one of eight still to be placed.

Unable to take in so much so fast, we said we would call back. We didn't have the money to fly from Massachusetts to Colorado on such short notice. We wanted the child but were put off by the need to make such an important decision so quickly. We had some clothing Ronald had outgrown, but not even an extra bed.

We had a list of questions when we called back. Could they fly Hoāng to us with some kind of escort? Could they somehow give us a few days to get organized emotionally and physically? The social worker finally agreed to find a family the child could stay with for the weekend. And yes, he would be flown to Logan Airport in Boston on Monday.

As soon as I hung up I realized I would need child care for Hoāng. Six weeks of school remained before summer, and as a junior-high art teacher in the Middleboro school system, I would not be home before 3:00. I called a dear friend. The last detail, I thought. She was thrilled to take on the job.

Despite the comfort of these arrangements, I felt an underlying pressure and apprehension because of the speed of events. Still, we felt good about having made the decision.

I turned to David. "I can't wait to tell the children!"

LOGAN AIRPORT

Monday, May 19, 1975

The sun winked at me through the front-door window as I bounded down the stairs. Mildred, our cat, scooted out of my way as I hurried to the kitchen. I looked at the clock—7:30 A.M. It was Monday, I had taken a day's leave from my job. I was going to be a mother again!

The children were so excited! This was the big day!

Kristen came through the door with a fist full of flowers. "Mommy, do you think Hoāng will like these?"

I drank in her image. Kristen was a pixie of a redhead. Eight years old, she had a turned-up nose and blue eyes. Her short curls caught the light from the kitchen window.

"Oh, Kristen, how thoughtful!"

Jessica frowned as she looked at her sister. Jessica was usually the generous, thoughtful one.

"Come on, Jess, the backyard is full of daisies. I'll help you find some," said Kristen.

Jessica, now five, had long straight brown hair, big beautiful eyes, and a darling "mushroom" nose that

David loved to nibble. People often thought all three children were adopted, they were so different.

Ronald came into the kitchen. "Mom, is it all right if I give Tiger to Hoāng?"

"Ronald, you love that tiger! Are you sure?"

He stared into the tiger's green glass eyes. Ronald, almost seven, had skin the color of dark honey. His cheeks and forehead were round, his upper lip soft as velvet. His black lashes curved in perfect half circles. He was a quiet child, very content, with a sense of inner peace.

I knelt down to look at him. "If you really want to, I think that would be wonderful."

David clapped and rubbed his hands together as he entered the kitchen.

"Let's go!" He held the door open, touching each head as the children filed by. Squeals and screams greeted the sun-drenched morning.

Logan Airport, Boston, Massachusetts; two girls, two boys, that's the way it should be, I thought happily to myself. We descended from the bright light into the Callahan Tunnel and the music from the radio faded.

David spoke toward the back seat. "You know, children, it's going to be hard for a while. Hoāng is going to be very upset for quite some time. Have you ever heard the term *culture shock?*"

"Culture shock?" Kristen leaned forward. "Isn't that when you come from another country and you find that everything in your new country is different?"

"Yes, that's right," David answered. The sun shone brightly as we came out of the tunnel. "Just think how many differences Hoāng will encounter."

"Do you think he's ever seen snow, Dad?" asked Ronald.

"No, I doubt that he has. What made you think of that, honey?"

"Oh, I don't know. I guess I remember being told that I hadn't seen snow in Alabama either." Ronald's head was pressed against the car window.

"And I doubt, too, that he's ever known a Christmas," I added.

"No Christmas?" Jessica almost fell between the two front seats, mangling her flowers a bit.

"Then there will be a lot of good things happening to him in this country," said Kristen. "Can I help teach him to read?"

Now all three heads popped up behind us.

"Remember how Daddy and I talked at the dinner table the other night? It's easy for us who have everything to think that this new brother is going to be very happy right away because he's had so little; but imagine yourselves flying to this country. Alone, no mother or father, speaking no English, wondering where you are going, wondering how long it will be before you'll maybe move again."

"But he's flying to us," said Jessica with a wry little grin. I turned and touched her face.

"Yes, honey, but he doesn't know that. He may have been told that, but he doesn't know us yet. You know, he's just five years old—your age." As we approached the sign LOGAN AIRPORT my stomach tensed a little. "It's incredible, kids, isn't it—all sorts of people flying all sorts of places!"

Like waves at the beach in summer, I thought—always pounding the shore when we arrive, yet they've been doing just that all winter.

"There's a plane circling to land!" cried Ronald. "Mom, how come I can't remember coming on a plane? All I remember is seeing how tiny the houses were from way up high."

"You were only three, honey. I can't remember much

myself before I was five. It's been more than three years since we picked you up at Bradley Field, Ronald."

"There's another one, and another," squealed Kristen.

"Let me see one! Let me!" Jessica pushed her way between the seats again.

"Stop pushing! You're crushing my flowers, Jess."

"Girls, stop it! We're here, now let's behave."

I was feeling amazingly calm and completely happy.

Inside the terminal, we began looking for Gate 9. We were forty-five minutes early. To the children's delight, we rode up the gleaming escalator, clutching hands, flowers, and Tiger.

"Oh, can we ride it again, please?" they all cried.

"Come on, kids," said David. "We'll ride it again after we pick up your brother."

We sat for what seemed a long time. That is, David and I sat. The three children, all in shorts and T-shirts, stood pressed against the enormous window.

"Take a last look at the threesome," I said to David.

"I'm looking. Believe me, I'm looking."

Turning to face him, I asked, "Are you nervous? You were the one who was so calm last time."

"I must admit I have some anxiety at this point; it's all happened so fast."

We stared down rows of brightly colored molded seats, orange, red, yellow, toward the children at the window. The exhaust from a departing plane distorted the sky as if an invisible fluid were moving the horizon over their heads.

Ronald's relaxed grip had allowed Tiger's nose to touch the floor. He turned to me. "Mom, how come I can't remember any mother but you?"

"Honey, you were so very young . . . ." No matter how wonderful and exciting an adoption is, I thought, there's always the reality—for some reason, a child has been separated from the biological parents.

"There's a plane coming in." David pointed.

The silver jet bounced the sun about an endless blue sky as it began its slow descent.

I approached an airline attendant. "Pardon me. Is that the 707 Delta flight arriving from Denver?"

"Yes, ma'am."

The terminal door kept opening and closing; the piercing whine of the jet stopped further conversation. Tension and excitement escalated!

"The movie camera! Have you got the movie camera?"

"I've got it," said David.

The door of Gate 9 opened; a large tube was readied. Like some accordioned umbilical cord, it slowly moved into position to connect our lives to that of a little boy from so far away.

"Dad, how will we know him when we see him?" shouted Kristen.

David spoke as loudly as he could. "Don't worry. They'll be looking for us! The airline has provided an escort to bring him to us."

The noise from the taxiing jet matched my excitement. People began to pour through the gate. Shouts of "Hello" and "There she is" broke forth as, one by one, people were recognized and united.

A rather large woman in a blue airline uniform appeared in the doorway with a little boy in tow. My eyes focused on him. The child looked Vietnamese, but he certainly was a large five-year-old. A nervous expression on his face, he huddled close to the woman.

"That child is from Vietnam," said David. "He must be older than five, though."

There were no other Vietnamese children about, so David went up to the woman.

"Are you looking for the Purdys?"

The young boy glanced apprehensively about. His amber eyes slanted down at the corners as sharp black pupils carefully looked us over. Clinging tightly to the escort's hand, he stood there in sneakers, cut-offs, and striped T-shirt. His hair had been all but shaved off. Chopped places revealed his scalp. Hoāng's hands, knees, and feet were oversized for his body. Like a puppy, I thought, his potential size yet to be realized.

The woman answered in a heavy accent. "Purdee! Purdee! Yes! These es Wang, Wang Quan Nguyen." Her red lips carefully enunciated every word.

She held up his wrist for us to see his plastic bracelets. One read, Hoāng Quan Nguyen, Saigon, Vietnam. The other, Hoāng Quan Nguyen, Denver, Colorado.

"The spelling is right, even if her pronunciation isn't. It must be him." I knelt to look into his face.

I couldn't belive the size of Hoāng! We had assumed that since he came from an Oriental background he would be small.

"Am I right that he speaks no English?" I said.

"No Englais. He speak no Englais. Ef he needs bathroom, he say 'diee.' He say 'bah e ma,' he mean father and mother." She bent down and spoke to Hoāng. "Bah e Ma." She pointed. "Thees es Bah . . . Thees es Ma."

Hoāng smiled nervously, revealing some very rotted baby teeth. He was every bit the size of Ronald.

"Ronald, would you like to give your new brother the tiger?" I said.

"I go now," said the escort. I had the distinct impression she was saying she was from Malaysia, but her English was so broken I wasn't sure. She seemed to soften as she placed Hoāng's hand in mine and looked me straight in the eye. "Reemember, thees boy es beene through a lot. Bee patient with im." She placed a shoebox of possessions in our hands, and we were alone.

"Here are some flowers," said Kristen, holding out the wilted daisies.

"Here," said Jessica, offering hers, her blue eyes riveted to her new brother.

Ronald hesitatingly held out Tiger. The three children laughed nervously as Hoāng took the tiger, flipped it over and, with the edge of his hand, pretended to cut it down the middle.

The smile on Ronald's face dropped. He looked at me.

David straightened up. "O.K., kids, let's go. It's time to go home."

Hoāng, holding David's hand, walked between us. The six of us meandered through the terminal, bumping into one another, five of us glancing at our new addition.

The three children caught sight of the escalator and were halfway up before David and I reached it. Hoāng's apprehension soon vanished. He quickly shot from between us to join the others. They ran to the top and back down again, not wanting to get off. After about six rides up and down, with movie taking and plenty of hand waving, we convinced the children it was time to go.

As we approached the car, Hoāng excitedly said something in Vietnamese. He jumped in the front seat and immediately turned on the radio. We closed the car doors as the radio blared.

"Oh, boy, do we have an active one!" David commented as he turned the key in the ignition.

The three heads were all lined up again, eyes glued to their new brother.

Once again we descended into the tunnel. There was considerably more traffic now as we slowly moved through the merging cars. Hoāng tumbled over into the back. Ronald made haste to move farther into the rear of the station wagon. In a flash, Hoāng rolled down the side window and hung halfway out. Waving his hands in stop-go fashion, he proceeded to direct traffic in Vietnamese.

FEAR FACES

When Ronald, Kristen, and Jessica came home from school, they immediately ran upstairs to see Hoāng. I glanced at the kitchen light fixture, expecting it to start swinging. Chaos had been normal fare since Hoāng's arrival.

The Emersons had just called, asking if they could stop by to meet our new son. After a full day of teaching, I desperately wanted to climb into a hot tub. I wondered why I had said yes, realizing that my real concern was their son, a difficult hyperactive child. Perhaps they would have some words of wisdom for me.

I heard cars pull into the driveway. I dug my toes deeper into my slippers and pushed myself to my feet.

"Hi there!" I opened the screen door. "I see you brought Paul." I watched their son dash for the swings.

"Congratulations," squealed Sue as we embraced. "Is it all right if he plays outside while . . . "

"Pam, this is fantastic," Bob broke in. "I just had to stop by when I heard the news. You and David are doing a wonderful thing."

"Thanks for the praise, Bob, but we really didn't hesitate."

26

"I can't wait to see him." Sue squeezed my hands.

"Sit down, and I'll call him, but it may take a few minutes. He's in the playroom." I went to the stairs. "Hoāng, honey, come downstairs. Some people are here to meet you."

"Does he understand you?" asked Sue.

"No, I'm sure he doesn't, but if he's ever to learn English, he'll have to hear it first."

Hoāng peeked around the corner, giggled, closed his eyes, and felt his way down the steps. Like an ostrich, I thought; maybe with his eyes closed he felt he could not be seen.

"Hi, Hoāng," Bob greeted him.

Slowly Hoāng approached Bob and crawled into his lap. A sing-song stream of Vietnamese filled the air.

"Oh, he's darling," said Sue. "And so outgoing."

Outgoing! I thought to myself. If they could have seen him in the playroom ten minutes ago!

Hoāng's attention was fully on Bob's face; his hands explored every feature. Bob sat motionless. It was as though he might scare away this strange creature if he were to move too quickly. Suddenly Hoāng's hands yanked Bob's heavy eyebrows.

"Ouch!"

"Hoāng, honey, don't hurt Mr. Emerson!" I lifted him from Bob's lap. "Why don't you go play with Paul?"

Hoāng placed his hands on Bob's knees and began searching his face. "Beer? . . . One dolla?"

Sue and Bob looked at me. The silence in the room spoke of our equal astonishment. Along with the humor, there was an instant awareness that this child was still on the hustle from his days in the streets.

"Paul is outside, honey. Why don't you go play? Swings, Hoāng, swings! Paul, look who's here!" I called as I guided Hoāng to the door.

The screech of the swings was all he needed to hear. I shielded my eyes from the descending sun. Every time Paul swung forward, his form blotted out its brightness. It pulsed and blinked on and off as the child swung to and fro. Hoāng bounded across the yard to meet his new friend.

"Pam, I must get back to work." Bob leaned over for a good-bye hug. "You have yourself a delightful child!"

Delightful, I thought. Images of GIs and the black market had been running through my head. Beer, one dolla?

"So glad you came, Bob. Sue, you can stay for some tea, can't you?"

"Sure, I'd love to. If you think we won't overdo it, that is."

We entered the kitchen and I reached for the teapot.

"Sue, Paul is big for his age, isn't he?"

"Yes, he's bigger than Peter now. He's taller, and at least ten pounds heavier, though Peter's two years older. Their personalities are equally different. Peter is very quiet while Paul tends to be more hyperactive."

"Well, he's met his match!" I set out some cups. "Hoāng is so large for a five-year-old. Before we picked him up at the airport, we had imagined some tiny starving waif. With the exception of his teeth, he really seems pretty healthy."

I poured the tea. The screen door slammed and Hoāng charged into the room, growling and grunting. Lips rolled back, upper and lower teeth exposed, he gave us what I called his "fear face." His expression and grunts were so primal, so animal! He charged, hands in a clawing position—and stopped three feet from me. A safe distance, I thought. I had seen our cat hold off many a dog in the same manner. Still, the sudden stampede unnerved me.

Paul's screams from the backyard broke the silence.

"Mom, Mom," he yelled as he burst through the door. "I have to go, I have to go! Where's the bathroom?"

"Paul, you always wait till the last minute," snapped Sue, grabbing frantically at his pants.

No sooner had she unfastened his jeans than a stream of urine shot out all over the kitchen. His screeching was horrible! Sue rushed him toward the bathroom.

I stared into my mug of tea and restrained a grin. At least there were other mothers dealing with hyperactivity!

"I'm sorry, Pam. He's so last-minute," Sue apologized when she returned from the bathroom.

"No problem." I tore off some paper towels and we both knelt to wipe up the floor. My aching body reminded me how exhausted I was.

"As soon as we clean this up we must be going. I'm really sorry."

As we threw away the towels I heard Kristen.

"Mom, Mom," she wailed. "Hoāng keeps bothering us!"

"I guess it's time," I said. "They've had enough interaction for one day."

I walked Sue and Paul down the driveway to their car. Kristen, Jessica, and Hoāng, all screaming, tore past us into the house.

"Thanks for coming, Sue. I'd better get back inside before someone gets hurt."

Bash! The screen door flew open and Jessica, propelled by a kick from Hoāng, sprawled out on the porch! That was it! I couldn't stand it anymore. I picked Jessica up but she continued to scream and cry as I checked for injuries. She would be fine, but I realized she could have been badly hurt. In an instant, I didn't care what Hoāng's past had been; I couldn't tolerate his behavior!

I stormed into the house, grabbed him by the shirt,

and dragged him kicking and screaming into the living room. He broke away from me and took a stand. Fear face and throaty grunts, he sliced the air karate style with his hands. A stream of hostile Vietnamese poured out. I could take it no longer! I picked him up and threw him on the couch face down. Tearing off his pants, I spanked his bare bottom! He screamed and gulped for air. There was no doubt I was communicating! I picked him up by the arms and turned him around.

"Don't you *ever* treat *me* or *Jessica* or *anyone* like that! You are going to *learn* to behave!"

Still unsatisfied, I dragged him upstairs and threw him into his room. His terrified look was making me feel very guilty. However, I had too much adrenaline in my system to care.

"Now you stay there until you're ready to behave!"

I descended the staircase. My legs wobbled. David and I had adopted this child! It had not been the choosing of our other three children. I clutched at the railing and made up my mind to call our social worker. I collapsed in the chair by the phone. My hand shook as I dialed the number of the Children's Aid and Family Service. I'll die if she's not there, I thought.

She answered and I began to cry. "I don't know if I can handle this, Freda. I've really blown my cool! I just spanked Hoāng and I've thrown him in his room. He is totally out of control." Fears that I was a potential child beater rippled through me. I had wanted to *kill* him!

"He tears around all day taunting and teasing the other children. He's a monster until David walks in the door; then it's all sweetness and light."

Before I could go on, she broke in. "You've done the right thing, Pamela. Don't berate youself. He must learn he is in a different value system! This is not the streets of Vietnam."

"Just last night I was reading that Vietnamese

children must be spoken to firmly in a soft voice." I wasn't crying now. I had gained strength from her affirmation.

"Pamela, the street life he has experienced has been a nightmare. Survival is all he knows! Use your intuition and forget the literature."

"But his hatred for me! His love for David. Swearing at me in Vietnamese!"

"How do you know he was swearing?"

"Believe me, Freda, if he had been speaking Swahili I'd have known he was swearing!"

"Sounds as if he has tremendous maternal anxiety. I'm afraid you are the target. He doesn't want a mother!"

I knew she was right, but the social-worker jargon!

"Please call me any time. And let's get together for a home visit very soon."

Idealistic images of what I, as a mother, and we, as a family, could provide had evaporated. I thanked her and confirmed a home visit. I hung up the phone and slumped in my chair.

Fear and anger seized me. Had I taken on too much? Could I handle it? What more would I encounter? I was clearly peering through a different window, a window into the ravaged past of a child's life, a past so different from the middle-class life in which I had been so tenderly raised. What chaos had I brought into the other children's lives?

Images from an old movie, *Inn of the Sixth Happiness*, flashed through my mind. Ingrid Bergman, taking in oodles of Chinese orphans, had moved me so deeply. According to Ingrid, all they needed was a bath, some food, and love. How simplistic it all seemed now!

As people of faith, we had taken on one of God's children. But now I was forced to recognize my anger. Lord, help me to love him, I thought. I know you do, even if I can't. Prayer and faith had gotten us into this, and I prayed would get us through!

31

MEMORIAL DAY WEEKEND

May 31, 1975

The weather was beautiful. It was unusually warm as we traveled along the mid-Cape highway that Saturday afternoon. Plans for a family reunion had been in the works for some time now. Memorial Day weekend on Cape Cod at my mother's house was shaping up to be a big event. My twin, Penny, and her family, my other sister Sally, and our grandfather and aunt planned to attend.

Hoāng's arrival had been so sudden, we now had mixed emotions about the trip. On the one hand, it would be fun to introduce him to the family; on the other, the trauma and culture shock he was experiencing were certainly not going to be eased by this gathering.

I turned to David. "You don't think he imagines we are taking him somewhere to leave him, do you?"

"Look," said David, "as the social worker said, we have to continue our lives just as we always have. Only time is going to make it clear to him that he is in this family to stay."

"Yes, I know you're right. It's just so frustrating not to be able to *tell* him he's here to stay."

"At least we'll be in our own home part of the time,"

said David. He added, "Your prediction is certainly coming true."

"What prediction?"

"Oh, your prediction about our summer home—that some day we'd fill it up with children."

Our summer house in Harwichport was about a mile from my mother's. We had purchased the "handyman's special" in 1965 before we had any children. A huge rambling farm house, initially it had no heat and was in much need of repair. This house was ours, the only one we'd probably ever own. I had gotten into the habit of calling it our common denominator. No matter how many parsonages we lived in, in the back of our minds we knew we had a permanent residence.

"Nia ca moin yoi, yah yadda yamma so. Noma ne e sin si din sin some . . . vay no loni yong . . . " were the sounds of the words Hoàng sang while the other children attempted to join in.

"I'd love to know what that song is about," I said. "It's amazing how the other children pick up the words and sing along."

"Oh, I wouldn't be surprised if it were some kind of national anthem. It sounds rather patriotic."

We pulled into our driveway in Harwichport. The trip hadn't been too bad, probably due to the fact that a bunch of bananas plus two boxes of cookies had been consumed. At any rate, during the one-hour trip, David had found it necessary to stop the car only twice to settle arguments.

"Okay, kids," said David. "Everybody carry something."

The children squealed as they grabbed their suitcases. Hoàng, empty-handed, raced ahead.

"So you're worried that this might be too much for him?" queried David as he looked for the house keys.

He unlocked the back door. Hoāng shot ahead as the four children stampeded through the house.

"Too much for *whom* should have been my question," I answered.

The smells of Cape Cod filled my senses—the familiar aroma of the pine-stuffed pillows in the bedrooms, the bayberry sprays in the kitchen, the bottles of shells on the kitchen windowsill.

Just off the kitchen in the back hall was an old captain's stairway, an intriguing staircase with a trapdoor at the top. This special place had been claimed by the children. They called it their airplane and would sit for hours in semidarkness, imagining themselves far above the earth.

"I want to show him the airplane," cried Kristen.

"No, I do," yelled Jessica.

"I'm the pilot," argued Ronald.

Just then Hoāng threw open the trapdoor upstairs. The three children looked up at his giggling face. It was obvious that no one was going to show Hoāng anything. He really was devilishly adorable.

"Look, we have a few hours before supper," said David, putting his hands on my shoulders. "Let's walk over to the cranberry bogs and let the kids work off steam. Tomorrow the relatives arrive. Let's take it easy while we can."

Hoāng ran around the house twice before we all crossed the street to the bogs.

Later after dinner, I called Mom to let her know we had arrived. Her voice was cool. I was certain that as I was explaining that "tomorrow would be soon enough for Hoāng to meet the clan," it was soon enough for her as well. Fear of all the unknowns, I was sure, had upset her.

At 10:00 the next morning, the phone rang. I answered.

Penny and her husband and three children had arrived at Mother's house. Penny and I, fraternal twins, were closer now than when we were younger.

"Pammie, Mom is a little nervous about this," Penny said. "She's really hoping you've done the right thing."

"I know she is, but you know she felt the same about Ronald. Just think how she loves him now!"

"I know. She'll be fine. We're all dying to meet him! Can we come over after lunch?"

"Sure." We planned for 1:30.

Before that hour arrived, the children had been fighting. Hoāng had wanted to take over every bedroom and toy, and had a miserable tantrum when he was thwarted by all of us, one after another. He was sobbing on his bed when the gang arrived.

David spoke firmly to me. "You go down and sit with your folks while I try to get things under control up here."

"Okay, honey. Kristen, Jessica, Ronald! Your cousins are downstairs. Let's go down and say hello!"

"Hi, Mom, good to see you." I knocked her glasses askew as I leaned over to kiss her.

"Hi, dear. How's everything?"

"Mom, everything is going to be all right. Hoāng has been through a lot, you know. I guess the hardest thing is not being able to communicate."

"Yes, I'm sure it will all take time," she said.

"Uncle Joe! Aunt Penny!" shouted the kids. A pandemonium of hugs and kisses broke out. Christopher, a strawberry-blond 9-year-old, was the oldest cousin; then Stephanie, 8, a flaming redhead like her mother; and Alex, 3½, a shy youngster.

"Aunt Pammie, where's Da Nang?" shouted Stephanie.

"Hoāng, honey. His name is Hoāng. He's upstairs with Uncle David. He's had a rough morning, and it may be a few more minutes before you can see him."

"Hey, honey," David called. I went up the steps two at a time. Then I heard David and Hoāng laughing.

They were playing with a green foam ball. The foam was so soft it could be crushed and completely hidden in David's hand. He would change hands behind his back, then Hoāng would guess which hand. If Hoāng guessed right, David would simply open his hand and let the ball spring into the air.

"Come on, Hoāng," said David. "Let's go downstairs and show your cousins."

Hoāng took David's hand and we made our way to the living room. Showing Hoāng the ball, he continued the guessing game. His eyes half on the ball and half on the gathered audience, Hoāng's attention broke. He ran out of the room, only to reappear on the stairway, making silly faces. In and out, to croons of "Oh, he's so cute," and "Isn't he adorable," it finally happened. Hoāng reappeared, took his stand, growled, and produced his most frightening fear face.

Then he quickly ran upstairs. Just what my mother needs to see, I thought.

"Dad has some candy bars for us," Chris told David.

"Hoāng would like that," said Ronald, looking as though he would like some himself.

Uncle Joe pulled out seven candy bars and led the parade up the steps.

"Hoāng, Uncle Joe has something for you," shouted Jessica.

Hoāng came out into the hallway. Uncle Joe, followed by the rest of the children, met him at the top of the stairs. Uncle Joe began passing out the candy bars, one by one.

"I'll bet he wolfs it down," I thought to myself. But instead of devouring it, he shoved it in his pocket. I watched him carefully eyeing the others' candy. As the circle of children unwrapped the bars—quickly, before anyone had a chance to protest—Hoāng had snapped off a good chunk of each one and shoved the big chocolate pieces in his mouth.

"Hey, cut it out!" a chorus of voices rang out.

"It's okay," soothed Uncle Joe. "I have more in the car."

"I'm sorry, kids," I apologized. "Hoāng has gone without an awful lot in his short lifetime. He's probably never seen so much chocolate."

"Why don't we meet you at the beach?" Penny suggested.

"Great idea!" agreed David. "It's warm enough to swim, and we can have a baseball game."

My mother, Penny, Joe, and kids left. The expression on my mother's face was still strained. She looked as if her worst fears had been realized.

She turned for a last word. "Don't forget, honey, be at my house at 6:00. Your grandfather and Aunt Cherry will be here by then. And I'll be meeting Sally's plane at 4:00."

During the next half hour I wondered what Hoāng's reaction to Nantucket Sound would be. At 2:30 the beach was beautiful. The clan was already spread out on the sand when we arrived.

"Hi," said Penny. "The water is unusually warm. We've already been in."

Kristen, Ronald, and Jessica headed toward the water. I bent down to slip off Hoāng's shorts.

"He can go in his underwear," I said.

Like a bullet, he was in the water face down, flailing about. I panicked! I thought he was drowning. I rushed in to pull him out, but it turned out that I had only interrupted his fun. Right back in he went, and under like a sea otter. His honey-colored skin was smooth and gleaming as he submerged and tumbled about.

Alternately, skin and white underpants rolled and reappeared.

"You sure have yourself an active one," commented Penny, one hand cupping her eyes against the sun.

"No kidding! David and I think he probably flew the plane here himself!"

"He must have learned to swim in Vietnam somewhere," said Penny. "He's certainly not afraid of the water. If he only spoke some English, I'm sure he could tell us a great deal, poor kid. How do you communicate, anyway?"

"Hoāng's the one who does most of that! He's incredible, the way he uses sign language—that, along with his facial expressions. He's really amazing. You watch; you'll see."

The cousins had banded together to build an enormous sand castle. They were digging huge holes near the water's edge.

"Concua!" shouted Hoāng. He sprang from the water and landed in the middle of the excavations.

"Concua, concua," he continued to shout. Little hands dug through the wet sand, surfacing with a beetle-shaped crab. He dropped it. As if in quicksand, it disappeared and he quickly ferreted it out again.

"You know, the kids and I have been coming here for years, and I never knew there were crabs like that!"

"Yet! Concua," Hoāng nodded his head and continued a long discourse in Vietnamese. All I could do was smile. He quickly went back to his digging. The children gathered about him, echoing some "Oh, that's gross" and "Let the poor thing go" responses.

At 4:30 we decided it was time to go. We had to shower and be at Mom's by 6:00.

Hoāng didn't want to leave. We kept trying to persuade him that it really was time to go. We pointed out his cousins, getting in their car. Then Kristen,

Ronald, and Jessica got into ours. Finally I picked up his pail of concuas. He began to cry. He screamed and wailed until his knees buckled under him. There he sat sobbing, halfway up the beach, facing the water. He seemed to be looking way out over the Sound. I gave him his pail of crabs. Vietnam is many miles away, I thought. I tried to console him. He swung at me and would have none of it. Finally, after twenty solid minutes of wailing, David carried the limp and exhausted child to the car. My nerves were shot!

The family reunion was well underway when we arrived. Mom seemed happy to see us. I put my donation of baked beans on the kitchen table and gave her a hug. It was hard to hide my feelings. I wanted to unload to my mother—let her know how hard it really was.

"Pammie," shouted Sally as she came into the kitchen. "So good to see you. Can't believe what you've done! Hear he's rather an active one!"

I could hear the commotion on the terrace as the kids mingled with the gathered relatives.

"Yes, you might say he's active. We think the war might have gone the other way if he had stayed in Nam!"

The two of us laughed and watched the cousins tear around the backyard. Sally slowly shook her head. A tall, attractive blond, two years older than Penny and I, big-hearted Sally was a sophisticated city girl.

"Aunt Cherry and Grandaddy are here. Come say hello!" said Mom.

Sally and I followed her.

"Pammie, dear." My aunt pressed her cheek on mine, kissing the air. "Mustn't ruin the makeup, you know. Let me look at you. I just want you to know how proud I am of what you've taken on!"

She seemed genuinely supportive and I loved her for it.

My grandfather slowly rose to his feet and spoke in a raspy voice. "I don't know how you do it, Pammie. You're incredible." A stately gentleman of eighty-six, bald for many years, he lived with my aunt in Connecticut.

"Oh, the photographer is here," shouted my aunt.

"Pammie and David, you don't mind, do you? I've hired a photographer to come and take a picture for the New Canaan paper."

Before I could answer, we were all being herded into the backyard for a photo. Finally in place around the picnic table—or should I say, all except Hoāng finally in place around the picnic table—we called, spoke, motioned to Hoāng to come and stand with us. Finally, David raced around the yard after him and held him in his arms, and a very wiggly, laughing Hoāng was photographed with the rest of us.

As the evening came to a close, my grandfather— great-grandfather to these seven children—stood up and called the brood around him. Hoāng stood smack in front of him. Grandaddy, hooking his cane over one arm, reached into his pocket and pulled out a roll of dollar bills. The children looked like chicks around a feed bag.

"Now, I want you all to salute! Atten . . . shun!" Grandaddy commanded. He stood erect, his right hand above his eyebrow.

The children all saluted. Then one at a time, each child was given a dollar bill. This time all eyes were on Hoāng as the children quickly stuffed the money into their own pockets!

A VISIT TO THE DENTIST

June 4, 1975

What a beautiful morning! Sun flooded my kitchen. As I sat with a cup of coffee, the face of a Cambodian child smiled at me from my UNICEF calendar. The child held a cup of milk to its lips. David and I had sympathetically supported this organization for years. Now it seemed that one such child had been catapulted over many miles into our very midst. Such irony—we now had a child who had traveled more miles and seen more of a deprived world than I would ever care to see.

Like some orbiting planet, he had now entered a new galaxy, as foreign to him as he was to it. He had cried himself to sleep the night before with a toothache. "Give aspirin for toothache," his papers said. How long had he been given "aspirin for toothache" and never been to a dentist? I had seen him spit pieces of his tooth on the sidewalk. How tough and yet fragile he was! He had survived a horrible war; few of us would have done as well. Yet now he was totally dependent on us—dependent on us to understand his sign language, his tears, his every need.

Like a planet, he was beginning a new orbit, only this time there must be control, there must be the time that nurturing requires. Beyond what we could give, there must be doctors, dentists, teachers, proper food.

The calendar reminded me; red ink spelled it out: *Hoāng dentist, June 4.* We would venture a little farther into the new world.

The office of our family dentist was just a short walk from our house. As we readied ourselves for the appointment, I reminded myself how terrific he was with youngsters. I called to the other children to inform them that Hoāng and I would be gone for about an hour.

Hoāng bounded out ahead of me. Mounting the stone fence in front of the church, he teetered along—like any child, I thought.

In the corner of the dentist's pine-paneled waiting room sat an enormous stuffed bear at least seven feet tall. The name Bruff was embroidered on his shirt. Hoāng was all over that flannel polyfill form in seconds. The black plastic eyes and nose were poked and rubbed and picked at. The green suede-cloth vest was lifted and stretched as Hoāng's head poked through the armhole. Bruff's protruding tummy became a launch pad for numerous flight attempts.

Knowing that probable tooth extractions lay ahead, I was pleased to see Hoāng so happy.

The dentist poked his head in the door. "You can bring your son in now. So, Mrs. Purdy, this is your new little one." He looked down at Hoāng through horn-rimmed glasses that magnified his large, kind eyes. "And what's your name, fella?"

"Hoāng is his name. He doesn't speak much English yet—just a few words."

The dentist patted the seat of the patient chair. Hoāng clung to me tenaciously.

"Oh, come on now," coaxed the dentist. "Look! See how the chair goes up and down!"

Hoāng grabbed for the button and smiled as the chair rose five feet into the air.

"Uh, that's enough. Now here, press this one." The dentist appeared relieved when the chair came down again. Numerous grins and nods in my direction gave me the feeling that the man was anxious to impress me.

"Now, how about a ride? Here, sit here." He once again patted the seat.

In a twinkling, Hoāng boarded the chair and smiled, exposing rotted teeth. The chair whirred up and down.

"Now, let's have a look at those teeth."

With clenched jaw and fists, Hoāng glared.

"Noooo," he screamed in the intervals between clenchings.

"Hoāng, let the dentist help you," I said. "He wants to help you."

Fingers dug into the sleeve of my blouse as Hoāng tried to hoist himself from the chair. I felt helpless, knowing there was no way out. His teeth desperately needed attention.

"Hey, look at this flashlight," said the dentist. He cajoled Hoāng by shining it in his own mouth. "See the . . . ite . . . n . . . mi . . . mout?" he garbled. The light bounded around magnificent white teeth, with the exception of some pure gold fillings.

This seemed to gain some cooperation. Taking a hand mirror, Hoāng riveted his eyes to the reflection of his own teeth. The dentist seized the opportunity to take a quick look. Even gentle prodding with his instrument brought forth blood.

The dentist's face communicated the terrible condition of Hoāng's teeth. In a serious tone he asked, "How old do you think this young man is?"

"Five. He's supposed to be five."

"He already has his six-year molars. And he has at

least two other molars that are so badly abscessed they must come out."

It was as if Hoāng understood every word. More screams and flailing ensued; it took both of us to hold him in the chair. The once starched white coat of the dentist was now wet with strings of blood and saliva.

"Mrs. Purdy, I think you should wait in the reception room. He will be less emotional if you're not here with him. Thanks to novocaine, he won't feel a thing."

I obeyed helplessly, with terribly torn feelings. What if he thinks I'm leaving him? His terror tore through me.

In the reception room I looked at Bruff, his clothes all askew; he was slumped to one side. I collapsed in a chair beside him. The tinkle of the bell on the door broke my trance.

"Hi. I came as soon as I could." Over the din of screams, David asked, "How are things going?"

"Oh, thank goodness you've come." I realized I was shouting to be heard. "He has at least two abscessed teeth. The dentist is going to pull them now."

The word *now* had just passed my lips when WHAP—Hoāng's sneaker hit the door.

David and I rushed into the room. The dentist was straddling Hoāng as if mounted on a horse. His glasses were crooked, and it was difficult to tell whose arms and legs were whose. It was clear that the pliers had found their mark and were not about to let go easily.

"Ah-ha!" The dentist's victory cry rang out! He held up the offending tooth.

Hoāng quickly grabbed his arm and bit.

"Owww." The dentist broke loose.

The decayed tooth had huge roots. It was black and partially broken off at the gum line. Hoāng examined the culprit of his pain where it lay on the table.

"Okay, okay, it's all over now," soothed the dentist. "Come pick out a prize."

From a cabinet, he withdrew a treasure chest marked For Good Little Boys and Girls. Hoāng wiped away tears with his sleeve and managed a grin as he pawed through various plastic rings, trinkets, and charms.

"Believe me, he felt no pain. I have never witnessed such terror. He must have been through a great deal in Vietnam."

"Doctor, maybe we ought to wait for the second tooth. I don't think *I* can take any more this afternoon."

"Yes, you're probably right. Meanwhile, I'll write you a prescription for penicillin. He will need to be on it for at least six weeks. Besides the two abscessed teeth, he has several others we may not be able to save. Fortunately, other than the six-year molars, they are all baby teeth. Still, he'll be needing them for several years to come."

"Hoāng, bite down hard on this cotton, O.K, buddy?" Dr. Sidney ruffled Hoāng's hair as we walked into the waiting room. Hoāng ran to Bruff for one last hug. Sitting on his friend's leg, he put on his sneaker.

Hoāng took David's hand, then mine, smiled and nodded, and led us out the door.

REFUGEE GATHERING

July 10, 1975

A s we drove along I carefully reread the newsletter from the Friends of Children of Vietnam.

YOUR FAMILY AND NEWLY ADOPTED CHILD ARE CORDIALLY INVITED TO ATTEND A DAY OF VIETNAMESE CELEBRATION AT THE CATHOLIC CHARITIES RETREAT HOUSE IN HULL, MASSACHUSETTS.

"Aren't there any specific instructions?" asked David.

I shook my head. "Hull can't be that big a town. We'll just have to ask."

It was hot and everyone had been irritable on the ride from the Cape. We usually did not leave Cape Cod during David's vacation; however, the invitation presented all kinds of possibilities. No day in our lives had been ordinary since Hoāng's arrival. We were eager to find an interpreter; perhaps some of our questions would be answered. What a day it could be for Hoāng—an opportunity to play with Vietnamese children! At the very least, it would be a fun day for our other youngsters.

Entering Hull, we quickly received directions. As we approached the retreat house we could see the ocean just beyond it. Children of every color, size, shape, from all parts of the world, were running about. It was an idyllic scene. It was also comforting that so many families had done as we had. A nun approached us.

"Welcome to Hull." Small, round, and radiant, she was dressed in a short white summer habit. David took her hand.

"Purdy is the name, Sister." Warm handshakes were extended and proper introductions made.

"This is Hoāng," said David.

"Hoāng, I'm so happy to meet you." She bent down, her crucifix swinging to and fro.

She led us over to two young women and introduced us.

"I'm pleased to meet you," said the tallest, her silky black hair switching in the wind. She and her sister, in their early twenties, were pure Vietnamese. Their eyes were perfectly almond-shaped, with no lid showing. By contrast, Hoāng's were more western looking, and his curly hair reflected his black heritage.

"How long have you and your sister been in this country?" I asked as we walked up the wide steps of the retreat house.

"Almost two year ago I came. My sister has recently just joined me. She speaks no English yet. We are living with a host family until we are trained well enough for job in area."

She bent down and spoke to Hoāng in Vietnamese. I was fascinated—not only by the sing-song quality of the conversation, but by Hoāng's enlivened reaction. Almost as if a bottle had been uncorked, he talked ceaselessly. All his uneasy, nervous expressions disappeared. He seemed freed from some unfair game in which he had been the ostracized victim. As the woman spoke, Hoāng stood erect, at full attention.

47

"Please, will you ask him some questions for us and interpret his answers?"

Our other children were only half tuned-in to what was transpiring. Since we were having such difficulty understanding the woman, we suggested that they go and play. They ran off, and we seated ourselves comfortably on the porch.

"Please ask him how old he is. We really think he's older than five."

She continued her sing-song speech. He answered.

"He say he do not know. However, Mrs. Purdy, I think you should know that in Vietnam if mother has boy child, she likely to say he younger than he is. In Vietnam all ten-year-old boys must go to army."

"Ten years old? I can't believe it!"

"Ask him what happened to his mother," said David.

Again they conversed. Hoāng's eyes lowered to the floor. I wondered how such a language could be understood.

"He say his mother took him to orphanage. She paid driver five dollar, all she had. They rode in . . . what you say . . . rickshaw . . . bicycle rickshaw, for two day and one night to the big house."

My heart was pounding. "Please ask him where he slept on this trip." She put her hand under Hoāng's chin and asked again.

"He say he and mother slept in rickshaw."

I hated to go on. "What was his mother's reason for giving him up?" David had his arm around me, trying to comfort me. I could feel the tension in both of us.

Hoāng's head hung low as he spoke. What agony for this child, now my child.

"He say his mother cry a little when she left. He say nun at big house say he must go to America because he have crooked eyes."

My heart was breaking for him and I hesitated to go on; but I knew I might never get another chance to speak to an interpreter. "Please ask him if he had any brothers or sisters."

"He say he had two brother, Ingh and Angh. He say they were with him to orphanage Colorado. Then American couple took Angh away. Brothers were younger than he. He say they always hold hand, but one day he went down to Coke machine, and when he come back, a white man and woman were taking Angh away. He say he ran after them, pulling on lady's dress. He ask if he could go with them. They say, 'Sorry, no.'"

I choked back tears and welcomed the wind in my face as I pinched my lips between my teeth. Hoāng pulled at the hem of his shirt.

"Do not feel too bad. They maybe were half brothers or two boys he care for. The need for family is great in an orphanage," she continued. "As for 'crooked eyes,' many mothers gave up their half-American children for fear of their lives. When French pulled out of Vietnam . . . how say . . . they took responsibility for their children. Many ships were sent by the French government to take away mixed children. Many French-Vietnamese children that did not get out were executed by the communists. The mothers never forgot this. It because she love him she gave him up."

Images of the slaughter of the innocents ran through my mind. Other parallels from Scripture sprang forth. Solomon recognized the real mother as the one willing to give up her child rather than have the child cut in two.

"He say he love his new parents and that he try to be good."

A bell began to ring. The more than two hundred visitors were being summoned into the dining room for a Vietnamese dinner. The interruption was unbearable!

"My sister and I must go now." The young woman rose. "We see you later. We must help in kitchen."

"Yes, of course, and thank you. Thank you so much," I said.

David shook her hand. "We appreciate this so much. We really do."

Our children flocked about us, and we began to maneuver into the hall. Wonderful smells from the kitchen filled the enormous room. Rows of long tables were set with silverware and chopsticks. We approached a family of five at one of the tables.

"May we join you?"

"Of course!" The young mother introduced her husband and gave the names and ages of their children—two boys and a girl.

"How do you do. Pam Purdy; my husband, David." I announced the names and ages of ours.

"How long . . . " we blurted out together.

"You first," I said.

"How long have you had Hoàng?"

"Since May, and you?"

"Since April."

"How are peer relationships with the siblings?" I asked, realizing how clinical I sounded.

"Well, they could be better . . . "

The little Vietnamese girl was a captivating child with wild blond frizzy hair and deep brown eyes. She was very thin and slumped down in her seat.

"Could be better? I know what you mean. Hoàng's adjustment is going to take a while."

"Oh, our little girl is doing fairly well. It's our oldest boy. He has the hard time." He had strawberry red hair and was a mass of freckles.

"Can I go to the bathroom?" he asked. "I see a sign over there."

"Sure. I'll take you," said his father, and he and the boy left the table.

"We have a wetting problem that began only after his sister arrived."

"Is that so?" I was almost delighted to hear of her plight.

"What's worse is that the other night he walked in his sleep—now that he is not here, I can say this. He walked into her room and urinated all over her head!"

Kristen, sitting nearest, spit her soup, unable to control her giggles.

"He did what!" I was straining terribly, trying not to laugh.

"The poor child woke up soaked. The boy said he had no idea he was doing it."

"Well, Hoāng has to be taken to the bathroom every night at 11:00 or he's wet in the morning."

Platters of food were placed family style before us—egg rolls, shrimp dishes, vegetable dishes of all kinds.

"Ughh . . . do we have to eat this stuff?" complained Ronald, wrinkling his nose.

"Just try it." David patted Ronald's knee.

"Isn't there any milk?" moaned Jessica.

"No, there's no milk. Have tea—that's what they drink in Vietnam."

"I like tea," said Kristen. "But where's the sugar?"

Suddenly it seemed very quiet. I looked down the table. There was Hoāng, plate heaped with food, grinning from ear to ear, mouth full.

Every time he took a sip of tea, he poured himself more. His cup was never empty. His orphanage life must have taught him that the glass that stays full gets the most.

EXAMINING ROOM NO. 4

August 7, 1975

Yesterday we received a letter from Friends of Children of Vietnam. As I read the letter I realized that three months had already passed since we had picked Hoāng up at Logan Airport. *Now* we were receiving this warning!

DO NOT ALLOW YOUR NEWLY ADOPTED CHILD TO BATHE WITH OTHER CHILDREN IN THE FAMILY UNTIL HE/SHE HAS BEEN CHECKED FOR PARASITES.

Why hadn't we received this letter sooner? Many, many times the children had all been in the same tub together. Copious health records had been mailed to us, but nothing about parasites!

"Examining room No. 4, Mrs. Purdy. You may bring your son right this way." The red-haired nurse led us down the hall. I ushered Hoāng after her.

"Where . . . go? What do?"

"The doctor has to examine you—look at you—before you start school."

"Everything off but the underpants," smiled the nurse. "Sit up here, son."

I handed the nurse the required stool sample.

"Shots? No shot! Please no!" Hoāng started to jump off the table.

"No shots, no shots, honey. The doctor is just going to check you."

I prayed that this visit would not turn into hysteria.

"Look at the cute pictures on the wall, Hoāng." His sharp eyes darted about. They focused.

On one wall in gold relief, a boy and a girl knelt at the base of a wooden crucifix. Hoāng looked at me and repeatedly shook his head.

"What are you afraid of, honey?"

Instantly a conversation with our social worker came to mind: "Do not be surprised if Hoāng is frightened by the symbols of the Christian faith. He may be Buddhist by background, and children are taught the differences at a very young age."

Not wanting to read too much into his reaction, I asked, "What is it, honey? What's the matter?"

Hoāng quickly slid off the examining table to the stool below. He placed one foot on top of the other and stretched out both arms. Using his fist, he reached over and pounded the palm of the other hand, then reached to the opposite side and pounded that one. He dropped his head as if hung on a cross, then looked up and shook his head—no!

The paper on the table crinkled and tore as he scrambled back up. Holding up one finger to obtain my full attention, he proceeded to cross his legs in a lotus position. Gently he placed the backs of his hands on his knees, and with his eyes closed as if in meditation, he sat in silence. He broke the trance by a quick nod of his head—yes!

I spoke very slowly, pronouncing my words carefully. "Did you sit this way in Vietnam?" I closed my eyes and placed the backs of my hands on my knees. "Did you sit often? Many times?"

"Yet, ee day . . . chaldritz . . . sonetime. Old men . . . many . . . in small house . . . sit long tine . . . long, long tine."

His papers said he had been in a Catholic orphanage since birth. We knew now that was not true. I wondered how much fabrication of details had taken place. No doubt those simplified statements had allowed quick and uncomplicated visas for these children.

Hoāng had clearly mimicked the differences in the Buddhist and Christian faiths, and he now seemed to slip into a deep meditative trance, still stitting in a lotus position, eyes closed. His hands, palms down, floated in front of him.

"What are you doing, Hoāng?"

At first glance I thought he was pretending to be blind. I had seen similar gestures one day while I was vacuuming. Hoāng had taken a section of pipe from the hose and was using it as a cane. He had tied one foot behind him with a jump rope, and I watched astounded as, with a coffee cup extended, eyes shut, he felt his way across the room. Here in the doctor's office, I was witnessing once again a bridge to Hoāng's past.

"Hoāng, honey! What are you doing?"

"Me touching . . . friends . . . Vietnam. They touch air . . . air touch me . . . we touch together."

I was terribly moved. A pang ran through me. This meditative dimension was not that of an American five-year-old. What would be lost through this up-rooting? Certainly, by my standards, he had gained much in the way of a secure family, medical attention, and all that a middle-class life-style could offer. But clearly there would be a loss of his cultural identity—an identity impossible to maintain.

The door opened.

"Well, who do we have here?" said the doctor.

The doctor was French, a soft-spoken man in his mid-forties.

"He is Vietnamese, Mrs. Purdy?" He gently wiggled Hoāng's knee.

"Yes, he arrived in late May, doctor."

"Does he speak French, do you know? Many people speak French in Vietnam, you know."

"I don't think so."

"Tu parles français, mon ami?"

Hoāng looked at me, shrugged his shoulders and said, "Me no know. Me Vietnam."

The red-haired nurse entered. "Here are the results, doctor."

He turned to me. "No parasites, Mrs. Purdy. Nothing to worry about; the specimen is clean."

Hoāng jumped off the table, dressed, and went into the waiting room.

A few minutes later when I entered, there he sat, surrounded by all the toys while three intimidated children huddled in one corner.

FOOLS FOR CHRIST

Sunday, August 19, 1975

The tension had been increasing between the children. Originally, it had seemed a good idea to put the two boys together. But Ronald's room had been completely taken over by Hoāng, as I discovered when I cleaned out the boys' closet. Waist deep, Hoāng had squirreled away egg cartons, boxes with bits of cereal inside. I even found stale rolls in a blue paper napkin. I remembered those napkins from a church potluck supper a month before.

Ronald was at a particular disadvantage in having to share the bunk bed with Hoāng. Ronald slept on top, and every time I tried to kiss him goodnight, Hoāng would tickle me from below, knowing I would recoil. Then when I kissed Hoāng, he would lock his arms about me with no intention of letting go. He wanted it to appear that I loved him more! The fact that Ronald had developed a stutter seemed an obvious symptom of stress, and David and I decided to separate the boys.

"I'm off to my 9:00 service," said David, his Bible and sermon in his hand, his robe draped over his arm. He leaned over to kiss me. "I have twenty minutes to get to South Middleboro; I have to fly. See you at 10:45."

David served two churches—one next door to our house; the other in South Middleboro.

"Please drive carefully." The thought of raising four children alone paralyzed me!

The only advantage to living next door to the church was the ability to walk. As soon as the children were dressed they could run off to Sunday school.

Kristen came out of her room. "This book has spit on it!" she screamed. She was holding the book by the edge with the tips of her fingers.

"Spit!" I exclaimed, looking at the slime on the book.

"I asked for it back and Hoāng said he wouldn't give it. I told him I would tell, so he slid it under my door with *spit* on it!"

"Hoāng! Get in here," I yelled. I grabbed him by the arm. "Did you spit on this book? You were asked to return it, not to foul it!"

Hoāng shrugged. "Me no know. Me Vietnam."

"Don't you 'me no know me Vietnam' me! You take this book and wash it off!"

Hoāng went into the bathroom.

"Mom, that kid is disgusting!" whimpered Kristen.

"Pull yourself together, now."

Hoāng came back, handed me the book, and I dried it with a towel. If there was anything Kristen valued, it was her books.

"Where did he learn such gross stuff, anyway?" protested Ronald.

"It's from what you call street life, I'm afraid." I glared at Hoāng. "As angry as he can make you kids, and me as well, we must realize that he had to be treated very poorly to exhibit such behavior."

"Who treated him poorly?" asked Jessica, coming out of the bathroom with a toothbrush in her mouth.

"Oh, other street kids. The younger ones learn from

the older ones. Hey, all of you! Finish getting dressed now! We'll be late for church!"

I had to admit that an emotional battle was raging inside me. I truly felt up against it! When Hoāng first arrived I had been so excited and proud of this undertaking. This morning I felt like a fool! It seemed that daily I was being besieged with anger, embarrassment, hostility. I had never known my full potential for those emotions! Over and against those feelings was the stuff I was really made of. I was an emotional idealist! A moralist who really believed in simple answers to very difficult problems. The answer was always love!

Where did I get that sentimentality! From my parents? I can remember my father, a staunch Republican all his life, choking up at the inauguration of President Truman. My mother? She selflessly took in and saw out of this world many an elderly relative.

The fabric of my childhood was made up of Roy Rogers and Gene Autry. They were never without their glass of milk! Father knows best and the innocence of Doris Day—was that the makeup of my psychological stuffing?

My thoughts were halted when Jessica entered.

"Honey, you can't wear that dress, it has a spot on it." I went into her room to find another. "Kristen, please stop feeding the fish! They were fed this morning."

Ronald pulled on my skirt. His expression showed he was near a breaking point.

"M . . . ma . . . mom . . . Hoāng keeps taking my underwear. H . . . he . . . has his own clothes, and he keeps taking mine!"

"Don't worry. There's clean laundry in the dryer." Getting ready for church was exhausting. I had often said we should have a dress rehearsal the night before.

"All of you, let's get some breakfast."

Hoāng had reached the kitchen first and was eating the last tangerine.

"I want a tangerine," said Jessica.

"Well, I'm sorry, honey, there aren't any more. Here, have some orange juice."

Hoāng took a section of tangerine and approached Jessica. I was so pleased to see this! She smiled and opened her mouth. He passed the section between her lips and popped it into his own mouth! Jessica burst into tears.

I grabbed Hoāng by the shoulders. "How can you be so mean!" I turned him around and swatted his behind. No sooner had I spanked him than I stopped and asked myself—how many times had another street child done the same to him?

I made it clear to Jessica that she would get a treat to pay for the injustice.

We finished breakfast, and Kristen and Ronald ran off to Sunday school.

I reached into the cabinet where I hid the lunch supplies and got out a small bag of potato chips. I admonished Hoāng for being so mean and handed Jessica the chips. I knew how much he loved this special treat! I also knew I had been reduced to playing his game. I really felt like Simon Legree.

Jessica smiled and opened the bag. Hoāng's eyes darted from me to his sister and back again.

"Now say you're sorry for teasing her with the tangerine."

I had fully intended to give him a bag of his own after an apology, but no apology was forthcoming. He very quietly went out the door. He was not easily broken! I knew it must be killing him.

After leaving Hoāng and Jessica at their classrooms, I

entered the church. This hour had become a time of deep reflection and prayer for me.

David read the Scripture lesson, I Corinthians 4:9, part of Paul's letter to the church in Corinth: "I sometimes think that God means us, the messengers, to appear last in the procession of mankind, like the men who are to die in the arena. For indeed we are made a public spectacle before the angels of Heaven and the eyes of men. We are looked upon as fools, for Christ's sake . . . ."

Hoāng certainly had a way of making Scripture come to life!

The service ended with the singing of "In Christ There Is No East or West." And on it went, "In him no south or north; but one great fellowship of love throughout the whole wide earth." I truly hoped this was so. I had so strongly believed it before Hoāng's arrival!

I stood and watched David walk down the aisle after the benediction. There was always fleeting eye contact between us at the close of a service.

Marilyn Harley and I met as we left adjoining pews.

Marilyn's hair is blond and beautiful. Her teeth are perfect. Her clothes are expensive and carefully chosen—chosen to mask a slight plumpness.

Marilyn's husband is barely her height. Soft-spoken, he has the face of a little boy. He rarely speaks.

They have two children, Donnie and Prudence. Pru was the image of Shirley Temple; Donnie, a Gerber baby for sure!

The light from the stained-glass window framed Marilyn's face as she spoke.

"How are things going?"

"Rough, I must admit. It's not easy. It's going to take time." I wanted to talk, to unload.

"Well, we admire you. But we sure don't envy you!"

I felt an expanding distance, a feeling of some kind of spacing, a telescopic jumping back as she spoke.

Marilyn handed Donnie to Henry as she led Pru down the aisle.

"Henry and I have often said that this is the kind of thing only people like you can do."

My jaw tightened. What could I say? Were not David and I members of the human race? Just because we were a minister and wife, were we better equipped to deal with tantrums, sibling rivalry, spit on books?

Just then Ron and Hoăng came up the stairs from Sunday school.

"Uppie-tairs. Here . . . papers," said Hoăng.

"Oh, Pam, they're so cute when they're little," said Marilyn with a grin.

Cute when they're little? Anger welled up in me. What about when they're grown up? Is it, I love kittens but I can't stand cats?

David was shaking hands at the door. An elderly parishioner was once again proclaiming that he looked just like the Pillsbury Dough Boy in his new white alb. She loved to poke her finger in his stomach, hardly the girth of the dough boy's.

"Good morning, Marilyn, Henry," said David.

"Good morning." They spoke in unison.

Pru did a sickeningly perfect curtsy.

Our four children appeared, indicated they were going home, and bounded out the door.

"As I was saying to Pam, David, we certainly do admire this undertaking. You people have a lot of courage."

"Well, thank you, Marilyn," said David. "It's an adventure."

"Yes. Well, you know God gives you only what you can handle. Right, Henry?" said Marilyn.

Henry was now holding both adorable Pru and baby

Donnie. All four Harleys beamed with their perfect faces and perfect teeth. They walked to their perfect car to return to their perfect house.

David and I stood in the framework of the huge white doors. We watched the Harleys drive away.

"Did you know they go to a restaurant every Sunday after church?" asked David.

"Oh, don't tell me any more. That family—especially Marilyn—why does she irritate me so?"

"She's too complete, too together. She thinks she has life all sewed up. But you know what? She doesn't."

"I know. I know she doesn't. But that bit about 'God never gives you more than you can handle.' That used to be one of my favorite sayings. I can't help thinking that the Harleys have never given themselves any more than they can handle." I paused. "I really don't mean to sound self-righteous. But the way Marilyn puts things really offends me."

"Who can you imagine saying that without giving offense?"

"Oh," I laughed, "maybe Mother Teresa."

KUNG FU KID

D avid and I had a 3:00 P.M. appointment at Union Street School. The school could not have been more conveniently located. Our parsonage was less than two blocks away.

We had agreed with the principal to allow two weeks of school to pass before having a conference regarding Hoāng's progress. He had encouraged us to place Hoāng in first grade because of his size and probable age. Our meeting this afternoon would include not only the principal, but Hoāng's teacher as well.

When we entered the school grounds, "after school" recess was in full swing. Children were tearing all about. There was a slide, a jungle gym, and at the base of a huge tree in one corner, boys were playing with matchbox cars. Buses began to drive up.

"Mom! Dad!" Hoāng emerged at full speed and threw his arms around us.

"Hi, guy," said David.

"Hi, honey." I was delighted with the affection.

"What doing here?" Hoāng tipped his head back to search our faces.

"Remember? We are supposed to see your teacher today," David reminded.

"Daddy and I will see you later, honey. You can walk home with Jess and Ronald. We'll be home soon."

"K.O." Hoāng shook his head.

"K.O.? What's that supposed to mean?" asked David.

"Run along now. Daddy and I will be late for our appointment." I turned to David. "I've heard him say K.O. before. He must think he's saying the opposite simply by reversing the letters."

"He really does seem pretty bright."

We entered the building and headed for the principal's office. I loved this school. It was a small, square, red-brick building. All the classrooms had been wall-to-wall carpeted for a quiet atmosphere. The principal greeted us and took us to the room where Hoāng's teacher was waiting. We sat in a semicircle.

"Here is a folder with Hoāng's work to date," the teacher said. "And by the way, the children really are having a hard time pronouncing *Hoāng*."

"I'm glad you brought that up," said David. "At home we have been calling him Hoāng Stephen. He has been called every foreign-sounding name in the book, and it really has been unsettling for him. He wants an American name. We feel, however, that he is Hoāng, so Stephen will really be his middle name. Someday he may want to go back to Hoāng—you know, for identity reasons. But I suppose we may eventually drop the Hoāng and just call him Stephen. That was the name of a dear friend of the family."

"So it's all right to call him Hoāng Stephen in school?" asked the principal.

"Oh yes, certainly," said David.

"As you know," said the principal, "Hoāng—I mean Hoāng Stephen—is getting extra help through Chapter 766. That law requires schools to provide for a child's special needs."

"We are aware of that," said David, "and grateful for it."

The principal spoke to the teacher. "Can you tell the Purdys how things are going?"

"Yes, well, things seem to be going pretty well when Hoāng Stephen is in a one-to-one situation. However, there does seem to be some difficulty when it comes to his peers."

"Isn't that understandable?" I felt the walls of defense building up in me.

"Of course it's understandable. I'm sure Hoāng has been through a lot. I asked you and your husband to meet with me today simply to let you know how things are going."

"What do you mean, when it comes to his peers?" asked David.

"Well, for instance, the playground is an interesting place to observe Hoāng. By the way, do you know where he learned martial arts?"

"Martial arts?" I asked, puzzled. "Do you mean karate?"

"Yes, he seems to have a number of the basic skills down pretty well. As a matter of fact, the children have nicknamed him the Kung Fu Kid. He does a pretty good karate kick."

It dawned on me that that very kick was what had sent Jessica through the screen door!

"Do you have any information about his schooling?" asked the principal.

"We have no information about anything. We only know that he was flown to Guam, where he received his immunizations, and then to Colorado to a makeshift orphanage. He was there about a month before being placed with us."

David snapped his fingers. "You know what? I'll bet that little song and dance he does—you know, the one where he moves sideways! I'll bet he was taught that as part of his training in the martial arts!" I was sure David was right.

"Well, he also knows how to use an abacus," the teacher informed us. "His math is a real strength. Naturally, numbers are a common communication. They are the same here as they are in Vietnam."

"We have done some tests on Hoàng," said the principal. "His I.Q. is in the superior range; on *some* tests it is as high as 134."

"That high?" I felt myself lighten with the news.

"He is a very bright youngster," the teacher added. "These tests are recommended for children his age, but from *this* culture. Now, if he can just learn to adjust, learn to adapt socially."

"We know," said David. "We know. It's all a matter of time."

I couldn't believe how encouraged I felt. I was filled with hope, sensing a distant vision of a bright, well-adjusted child!

We looked over Hoàng Stephen's work folder, noted that his desk was smack in front of the teacher's, and proceeded to give her as much background information as possible.

David and I left the building and, for the first time in five months, felt truly encouraged.

CHINNEYS AND SPIDERS

October 4, 1975

L eaves skittered across the kitchen floor of our house at Cape Cod, the wind helping to slam the door behind David as he entered.

"Honey, here they are! The pictures of our fishing trip!"

Impulsively, I put my arms around him and buried my face in his neck. I loved the smell of him. I felt very teary and needed strength and support. David instinctively knew when I had had it; there was no need for words. Sometimes we would just hold each other in silence.

"Come on, sit down. These pictures will cheer you up."

We sat on the couch and I began to look at the photographs.

"Look at this one of Jessica. Remember that pathetic catfish?"

"Where?" said Jessica, entering the living room.

"Oh, doe girl, look at this poor fish!" Slimy and barbed with horny fins, the catfish had swallowed hook and bait entirely. David had no choice but to cut the line and throw the poor thing back.

"Hey, Ron, Kristen, come see these pictures. Look at

these two turkeys with their lines in the bucket of fish!"
laughed David.

"Do you believe it?" I said. "Ronald, you must admit
those fish were at a slight disadvantage!" Ronald
giggled.

"Look at this one of the girls!" said David. Kristen
and Jessica were holding two tiny yellow perch and
beaming with joy. Upper Mill Pond glistened in the
background.

"This one—this one's perfect! Have you ever seen
Hoāng Stephen so happy?" said David.

"Oh, honey, it's marvelous. It's good of both of you! I
must have an enlargement made!" How incredible this
thing called a photograph—pure joy, frozen in time.
The picture showed a radiant Stephen with his father.
Clutched in a wet kitchen towel was a big yellow perch,
the biggest catch of the day.

It felt so good to hold some happy memories in my
hand. It had been a typically hard morning. Stephen
had left an antique metal train in the driveway. It had
been David's father's, but it had more than sentimental
value. David had backed the car out and crushed it. We
had both been terribly angry with Hoāng Stephen, who
was now in his room moping.

"I think I'll take these up to Stephen." Why did I
allow material loss to get such a grip on me? I picked up
the basket of laundry I had been folding and headed
upstairs.

Stephen was lying on his bed. I put the laundry
basket on the dresser.

"Hoāng Stephen, look what I have! Remember our
fishing trip?"

Stephen grabbed the pictures and broke into a full
grin. The one of him and David was on top.

"Oh goot!" Stephen pounded his chest. "Big fish! My
fish!"

"I'm going to have this picture of you and Daddy made bigger!"

Stephen carefully looked over all the pictures, examining them one by one.

I stretched out on Ron's bed. I loved this room; it had a steeply slanted ceiling, one large window, and another tiny four-paned one under the steepest part of the eaves. The boys' bunk beds were now twin beds. Stephen rolled off his and under Ron's.

"What are you doing, you little character?" I hung over the edge and pulled the bedspread up.

"Mom." Hoāng Stephen was now on his own bed.

"Yes, honey."

"In Veet . . . nam, another bed, up here." He was standing now, describing a bunk bed.

"In Vietnam, honey? In the big house? A bunk bed? Like you and Ron had?"

"Bunk bed. . . . Yet!" he said with a delighted expression. "Big house . . . Veet . . . nam. Two sleep top, two . . . bottom."

"What else do you remember about the big house, honey?"

"Many chaldritz. . . . Many boy, many girl. Boys on one side, girls on other."

With great animation Stephen was pacing the room, indicating there had been a partition between the two groups of children.

"Each bunk . . . " he ran to the curtains, "had this." He held up the net curtain and boxed in an imaginary bed. Mosquito netting!

"Yet, big house. . . . But there a small house too. A cook house . . . cook food."

"What was cooked in the cook house?" I asked.

"Gum," explained Stephen, outlining with cupped hands the shape of a huge caldron.

71

"Gum?" I repeated. I had not noticed that David had entered the room.

"Oh, he must mean rice," said David. "You know how it says Sub Gum this and that in a Chinese restaurant?"

"Rice. Yet, rice. . . . Gum, rice!" replied Stephen with short nods.

"How many times a day did you eat?" I spoke slowly, miming eating from a bowl with a spoon.

"One tin . . . e . . . day," he said, holding up one finger. "But night . . . night tine I go down to small house . . . cook house. I build big fire. . . . I cook much gum. . . . Eat all I want."

"You got up at night, in the dark, and went down to the cook house?" I said, wondering if this was possible.

"One tine . . . nun lock me in room uppie . . . tairs. Can't get out! I cry . . . yell . . . beat on door!"

"Then what happened?" I was totally enthralled by his animation.

"Find hole . . . little hole in wall. . . . I hit. . . . I make bigger. Soon big enough, I crawl through." Hoāng Stephen dropped to his knees and wiggled through an imaginary hole. "Then I crawl out!"

"What did the nun say when she saw you?"

"She yell, ohhh!" Stephen made a face, eyes wide with surprise, mouth wide open. "Then she went look at hole . . . and again, ohhh!" Hoāng Stephen cupped his face in his hands.

"She really must have been surprised!" I said.

"What else did you eat in the big house? Do you remember?" questioned David.

"Sontine, mother visit. . . . Bring dooey."

"Your mother brought you bananas?" A dooey had been described to me as a little green banana. At that moment it occurred to me that those may have been underdeveloped bananas, eaten too soon because of hunger.

"Nun took dooey. . . . Put up on shelf for me."

"Did your mother visit often?"

"No, not . . . often." Hoāng Stephen sat very quietly now, looking at the floor.

"Tell me more about the cook house," I urged.

"Cook house big," he continued. With side steps, arms outstretched, he indicated a large opening.

"A chimney?" I guessed.

"Yet, that it. . . . A chinney! Daytime we chaldritz . . . go up chinney, get . . . how you say . . . bugs?"

"Bugs? Spiders?" I fished for the right word.

"Spiders, yet! . . . Long legs . . . crawl in chinney. Fire . . . stove." He continued to outline with his hands. "We chaldritz . . . throw spider on stove, eat them. . . . Goot!"

I looked at David and froze my face, afraid my repulsion would show.

"You ate spiders?" I said it as calmly as I could.

"Yet! Goot! Taste like . . . how you say . . . popcorn!"

I was stunned by Stephen's survival instincts. When he ate a banana there seemed no way to keep him from scraping the inside of the skin with his lower teeth. He ate everything. If I served chicken, he would crack open the bones with his teeth and eat the marrow!

"Did you swim in Vietnam?" asked David.

"Yet! Big river . . . with . . . what you say, bridge."

"A river with a bridge!" I exclaimed, captivated by the scene he was describing.

"People diee . . . bridge," he continued.

David spoke. "Diee? You mean bathroom? People used the bridge as a bathroom?"

"Yet! . . . Bridge had seat. . . . Hole in seat . . .

se . . . mell!" Hoãng Stephen rubbed his nose and grimaced. "Hate that. . . . Here much better. . . . Here toilet paper. In Vietnam . . . me friends and I look for paper in street . . . candy paper, cigarette paper. . . . We use what we find."

I had to laugh, remembering Stephen's first encounter with toilet paper. I had walked in to find an entire roll unwound on the bathroom floor.

"So you like toilet paper!" I said.

"Yet. . . . Mom! Grandma Chatterton? Is she rich? She have so much toilet paper!"

I chuckled. "No, honey, she's not rich. She just likes to buy toilet paper when it's on sale."

The phone rang, hurtling me back to reality—or I should say, the reality I was presently living. Hoãng Stephen once more had taken us many miles away, to a place we'd never known.

As I lay on the bed, my eyes focused on the antique bureau between us. Scratched into the side of it, in huge letters, was the word *Hoãng!* The H was small, compared to the finishing G. It was one of my favorite pieces of furniture! The handles were carved wooden grape leaves.

My initial reaction was anger. However, I was still feeling the effects of our conversation; I said nothing. Was it wishful thinking to see those huge letters in a positive light? Could it be that he was making the statement "I am!"? I so much wanted him to feel good about himself, but it was so hard because of his behavior! I could yell, scream, and reprimand him into oblivion—the only message he would hear would be, "I'm no good. I'm bad." No, I must affirm him whenever possible! Hoãng Stephen was making a mark on me as clearly as he had scratched his name on the bureau!

HALLOWEEN AND
THE BOOM-A-LOOM MAN

October 31, 1975

I had just come home from school. It was 3:00 and getting very dark. Toward the west through my kitchen window, I could see blue-black storm clouds rapidly advancing over the church. The rays of the sun were still strong enough to slice through contrasting thunderheads. The ground below was a wash of brilliant autumn colors. Children shouted as they filed out of school. In coats of red and blue they shuffled through heaps of yellow leaves.

"What every artist wants to capture!" I'd been told many times. But not me. Nothing could reproduce the symphony going on before me—the sound and movement of wind, the sweeping shadows of renegade clouds rippling over the children as they rushed along the sidewalks. It was not to be captured; it was there for me to consume, to live in the moment.

One by one—Kristen, Ronald, Jessica, Hoāng Stephen—entered the yard and immediately jumped into the pile of leaves that had been raked the day before.

I picked up my mug of tea and returned to the window. In an instant the colors had disappeared. The clouds had thickened and the distant rumbling of thunder and crackle of lightning could be heard. I had just stepped out onto the porch when an enormous thunderclap caused me to jump, sloshing hot tea all over my arm. All the children screamed and ran toward me. When they reached the house their screams turned into excited shrieking! All, that is, with the exception of Hoāng Stephen, who was crying hysterically. Inside, he ran aimlessly about the living room and wailed ceaselessly. He collapsed to the floor, then ran to the window. I dodged his feet and caught him fast in my arms.

"Stephen, don't be frightened." I tried to hold him as he thrashed about. I spun into a chair and rocked him, attempting to deny his terror, which had once again become mine. Like one drop of mercury rolling into another, I found myself in the presence of his past—an experience so life-threatening I was reliving it with him.

"It's just a thunderstorm!" said Ronald. His face showed honest concern.

Another bolt hit! Through the living room windows we could see a yellow-white finger of lightning rip open the sky. Rain began to pound the tin porch roof. There was instant screaming! Ronald scrambled under a table. The girls clung to each other as Stephen and I clung together. His wailing was piercing! I jumped up. I don't know whether I could no longer stand the hysteria or it was sheer practicality. I knew only that the car windows were wide open and I had to go and shut them.

"I have to close the car windows, kids. I'll be back in a moment."

More thunder rumbled overhead as I dashed out to the driveway. Hoāng Stephen came running after me. He stopped at the porch. Between the intensity of the storm and his crying, I couldn't make out what he was trying to say. He kept pointing at the sky and jumping up and down. He was beckoning to me to come inside.

"I'm coming, honey. I'll be right there." Water ran in rivers down the sloping driveway. My shoes filled as I took giant steps back to the house.

"They come, they come!" Stephen made the shape of an airplane by locking his thumbs together and holding the rest of his fingers at right angles.

"No, no plane, honey. It's just a thunderstorm."

He continued to point and look in all directions at the sky. He pointed toward the church. Then quickly, studying his hands, he put them together and blew them apart. His sound effect of an explosion made it clear to me that he had heard and seen bombs fall!

I picked him up. I held him tightly and entered the house. I thought of the many Vietnamese mothers who had done just as I was doing—grab their children and head for safety. But I knew it was just a storm!

The pounding rain soon feathered off and danced down the street. The lights in the house dimmed, came back on, and the storm was over.

"I have a nature book that describes what a thunderstorm is in big pictures," said Kristen.

"Good, honey. Do hurry and get it. Maybe it will help."

Kristen was back in a moment. She opened the book and sat down next to Stephen. He wiped his face with his hand and looked at the pictures.

"See the thunderclouds forming?" said Kristen.

"No bombs, Hoāng Stephen. No bombs," said Jessica.

The phone rang. It was Stephen's teacher. What now? I thought.

"I'm calling out of concern for Stephen. Generally things have been going quite well. However, today . . . "

"Yes?"

"Today we had our Halloween party. Stephen wouldn't come into the room! At first I didn't know why. Apparently it was the skeleton on the door. I took it down, but unfortunately the children did tease him about it. I just thought I'd warn you, since tonight is Halloween."

"Thank you for the warning. Each day a new piece of the puzzle comes together. If you can believe it, we just lived through the bombing of Saigon with that passing storm. I'm still shaking from Stephen's hysteria."

"One more thing before I forget, Mrs. Purdy. Besides the skeleton problem, we had another incident. We had pumpkins and corn stalks in one corner of the room. It could be that Stephen is still in an oral stage, but he kept chewing on the stalks. He even offered pieces to the other children!"

"For once I know what that's all about. Day before yesterday the children and I went out to the garden to cut corn stalks for the Sunday school party. Stephen became very excited. He held a piece to his lips and then to mine, and said, 'Taste. . . . good!' I hesitated at first, but to my surprise it was sweet! I was then directed to the house and straight to the sugar bowl. I was told that children in Vietnam chew sugarcane every day to keep from being hungry. Now it's clear to me why his teeth are in such awful condition."

"That's really interesting, Mrs. Purdy. You ought to be writing all this down for Stephen."

"Yes, I should. I have written some things down. Again, thanks for the tip on the skeleton. I was planning to hang one myself. Maybe to lessen the fears I'll take the children trick-or-treating while it's still light out."

I hung up the phone. I shook my head. How we, as a

culture, play games with death and think nothing of it. I returned to a more peaceful living room.

"Hoāng Stephen, come sit on the couch. Your teacher just called. She was telling me about the skeleton on the door." Stephen's eyes widened.

"I no like skel . . . ton!"

"Had you seen one before?" I was almost afraid to ask. Kristen, Jess, and Ron listened intently.

"Yet. . . . Vietnam. . . . One night . . . me and friends . . . walk through field." His eyes were wide and his back straightened. "We cross . . . how you say . . . railroad tracks? There was a big hole . . . grave. . . . We scream! Skel . . . ton crawl out of hole and chase us."

"Are you sure?" said Jessica, cocking her head.

"We ran for barn. . . . Cows in barn. . . . But plane come. . . . Bomb hit barn. . . . Blow up cows."

There was no way of sorting out how much was fact and how much was fantasy.

"Did that happen on Halloween?" said Ronald.

"No. . . . No Hallo . . . een Veet . . . nam."

"What was the name of that man in Vietnam, Stephen? The Boom-a-loom Man or something?" said Kristen.

Hoāng Stephen smiled. "Boom-a-loom! Good man. . . . Fat man with big stomach. He eat so much his stomach like bowl . . . made of skin."

"This person lived in Vietnam?" I said.

"Yet. . . . He walk around. . . . Feed all chaldritz! His stomach full of noodle . . . how you say . . . spaghetti. He spoon spaghetti to us . . . from his stomach bowl."

Ronald stood up and acted out a mime of the Boom-a-loom Man.

"You mean his stomach is this big and he feeds children from it?"

"Yet. He walk around and feed all the hungry chaldritz."

Santa Claus and Superman sprang to mind. I guess it is very human for each culture to develop some superheroes. I made a mental note to speak to the other children about that later. The Boom-a-loom Man was probably pure fantasy. Maybe there had been a fat man who had shown some mercy to those children at one time. From a small child's view, looking up, it might have appeared that the man was feeding them from his stomach. I was fascinated by Stephen's imagination.

"Hoãng Stephen, I've heard you use the term *maguera*. What is a *maguera*?"

The other children giggled and put their hands to their mouths. Stephen grinned and shrugged.

"Mom, you don't want to know," said Kristen.

"Why, what is it?"

Ronald snickered. "He says if you look at a naked lady, your eye gets all puffed up and infected."

The three children went into gales of laughter.

"In Veet . . . nam, it true! I saw a man, eye all puffed out." Stephen closed one eye and screwed up the side of his face, trying to look grotesque.

"Everyone told us chaldritz . . . that man saw a naked lady!" Stephen shrugged and slowly shook his head. "Never look at . . . naked lady!"

I couldn't control myself. I had to join in the laughter! This child had brought such peaks and valleys to my life. In one afternoon we had moved from bombs to naked ladies. I thank God for those ups! The Boom-a-loom Man and naked ladies!

BATHTIME

November 18, 1975

tephen and Ronald splashed around in the tub. Earlier that evening I had made a charcoal sketch of Stephen. At his request, it was now taped to the bathroom mirror. Because Stephen was so active, it had been a difficult portrait to do, but I was pleased with the final result.

I left the bathroom to get the other children ready for bed.

"Blub . . . lub . . . lub . . . " Stephen loved to flop face down like a sea otter. He would submerge and surface as he rolled through the soapy water.

"Hoāng, cut it out," screamed Ronald. "Mom, Hoāng keeps splashing me."

I returned to the bathroom. "Please try to call him Hoāng Stephen, Ronald, or he'll never get used to the name. Stephen, stop the splashing this minute! Leave your brother alone!"

I headed for Kristen's room.

"Cut it out," yelled Ronald. "You're getting everything soaked!"

I stomped back into the bathroom, my anger intensifying with every step. Now Stephen was splashing water at Jessica, who was playing hide-and-seek behind her bedroom door, which opened directly off the bath.

"All right now, I've had it. Out of the tub this minute! Jessica, you get to bed!"

Soapy water was running down everything—the walls, the doors, even the charcoal portrait! It was ruined!

I felt my throat tighten. The portrait, intended as a study for an oil painting, was destroyed. I had done oils of the other three children; I had wanted the fourth so much. I didn't know whether to scream or cry!

But it was Stephen who suddenly began to scream *and* cry. I turned to see blood pouring down his arm.

Ronald jumped out of the tub, yelling "Ygh! Bloody water!" My anger turned to panic.

Calling David, I grabbed a towel and wrapped the bloody wrist. I pulled Stephen out of the tub; his body was limp with fear. He screamed until his breath ran out. There was dead silence. Then he gulped more air and screamed again.

David came running up the stairs. The girls rushed into the bathroom.

"He's cut himself on something in the tub!" I reached carefully into the bloody water and pulled up a broken glass.

The other children were no help.

"Yuk, he's all bloody."

"Is he going to need stitches, Mommy?"

"Does he have to go to the hospital?"

With each question the screaming grew louder. I wanted to brain them for opening their mouths.

"David, dress him warmly. I'll see if I can get someone to stay while we're out."

The screaming continued. "Are they going to cut me open and pull out a baby?" Stephen cried out between huge gulps of air.

His terror-filled eyes were like a window into another time, another place—a place of war, fear, hate. What had this child seen and heard?

We set out for the hospital, David driving, Stephen screaming into my coat as I held him and tried in vain to comfort him. My very ribs vibrated with the wailing, forcing tears from my eyes. I had never witnessed such human terror. As my eyes met David's, I knew mine mirrored the fright I saw in his.

Emergency room doors were flung open; all eyes fixed upon our noisy entrance. A nurse quickly directed us to one of the examining rooms.

"Don't touch me! Don't touch me!" Stephen kicked and screamed as two nurses tried to hold him down.

A doctor came and unwrapped the bloody wrist.

"What did he cut this on?" He shouted, in competition with the din.

"A glass. He must have taken it into the tub with him." I looked at the gash in his wrist.

"It will have to be sewn up," said the doctor.

The skin on Stephen's hands and feet was thick and tough. I had often been amazed at the lines and wrinkles around ankles and toes, knuckles and fingers. It was like looking into the past. I could see the imprints of generations of peasants in rice paddies. Stephen also did an amazing trick with those fingers. He could bend them back to touch his wrist. It was as though he had elastic for cartilage.

"Hoāng Stephen, the doctor wants to help you! He has to close the cut." Tears were still rolling down my face. It must have been obvious to the doctor and staff that my husband and I were emotionally exhausted and unable to quiet the child.

"Why don't you and your husband wait outside?"

"No, no! Don't leave me! Don't leave me!" Stephen's

fingers were like a cat's talons, locked into the cloth of my coat.

"Daddy and I will be right outside. We won't leave you. Please, Hoāng Stephen, let them help you!"

"You'll see our feet under the curtain," David told him. "We won't leave you."

David firmly squeezed my arms to indicate it was time to leave. The strength of his hands was comforting, and at that moment I was sure it was the only thing holding me together. We stood outside the curtain, trembling, as the screams continued.

We heard Stephen yell, "Me want to watch! Don't touch me unless I watch!"

"You mustn't watch," said the doctor. "Now, now—look away, and we'll be done in no time."

"No, no! Me have to watch. Have to!"

"All right, all right." The doctor finally gave up. "But you must hold that hand very still . . . very still."

We peeked around the curtain. Stephen was sitting lotus style, holding the injured wrist with the other hand as he sobbed and cried.

"Just a little novocaine now. Hold still."

"No, no!" again pierced the air.

"Darn! Nurse, get me a sharper needle! *Hold still now!*" The doctor was getting angry. "Now, now, that doesn't hurt. We'll be done in a few minutes. . . . Darn! . . . I need another needle!"

As Stephen's wrist was being bandaged, the doctor stepped out to speak with us.

"Your son has been through a lot. I don't mean just this cut, either. I have never seen such fear and lack of trust in a child. How long has he been in this country?"

"Almost six months," David answered. "He's a survivor, doctor, and I guess to be a survivor, you can't afford to trust anyone."

"Do you think he'll ever adjust?" I asked, feeling weak. I looked for a chair and sat down.

"He needs love and lots of time. You folks are exactly what he needs."

Stephen emerged, bandaged and fully dressed, the flush of tantrum and tears still about his face. We made an appointment to return in five days to have the eight sutures removed.

Three days later we cancelled. Hoāng Stephen had come downstairs beaming, to show us his outstretched hand.

"I pull out spiders all by myself!"

FIRST CHRISTMAS

December 13, 1975

I t was a tradition to put up our tree about two weeks before Christmas. On a Saturday, we would buy the tree, decorate, and enjoy together the excitement of Christmas. It was a cherished family time.

This year would be Hoãng Stephen's first Christmas. We all were excited for him. The first snowfall earlier this month had proved a sheer joy. Clad in a heavy blue snowsuit, boots, hat, and gloves, Hoãng had ventured cautiously out—like a man on a strange planet, I thought—only to run back to the door and, with mad sign language, ask if he could lie in it.

"Of course," I had said, and the five of us watched him bellyflop, kick, taste, and roll in the beautiful white stuff. Kristen, Jessica, and Ronald had imitated his antics as if they too were experiencing snow for the first time.

David opened the back of the station wagon. "I think we'd better take the tree in through the front door."

"Kids, run in and unlock the front door from inside." We rarely used the front entrance, but it had the largest opening. I pulled my coat around me. It was cold. My feet were frozen.

We dragged the tree through the unshoveled snow. The children squealed as it was pulled, trunk first, through the door. Hoāng Stephen picked up a broken pine bough and danced in circles around the living room.

I put on a kettle of water for hot chocolate, then placed the cartons of Christmas ornaments on the coffee table. I felt sentimental about the boxes themselves. They were fresh-fruit containers from Oregon, reminders of friends and their gifts from past Christmases. Each box had individual sections, just right for holding the precious ornaments.

"Here are some popcorn and cranberries for stringing, kids. I'll get the needles and thread."

"Mom, Hoāng Stephen keeps eating the popcorn!" shrieked Kristen as I reentered the room. She had cupped the bowl to her chest and was glaring beady-eyed in his direction.

"Show him how to string it," I said. "Look here, honey. First you put the needle through a piece of popcorn, then a cranberry, and so on."

David reminded them, "Don't forget, kids. He's never known a Christmas before!"

Stephen dropped the popcorn and went quickly to the boxes of ornaments. No sooner did I secure the safety of one treasure than he would grab another. Each ornament went right into his mouth.

I surmised that because of his past life he relied heavily on touch, taste, and smell. Or was it an unsatisfied oral fixation? It was the same with each object he had encountered over the past few months. If he opened a door, his mouth was on the doorknob. If he touched something, he either smelled his fingers or pressed the object to his face to inhale its odor. He delighted in chewing balloons and rubber toys. Though this habit was very annoying, we had tried to

87

understand that it was Hoāng Stephen's way of learning about his new world.

"Here is the crèche. I'll put the box on this side table," I said. Kristen and Jessica opened it and began to assemble the small figures.

"Hey, Kristen. Remember this?" Ronald called her attention to a styrofoam shape from one of the boxes.

"Oh yeah! Remember that, Jess?" said Kristen. The three of them grinned at the photograph in the center of the ornament, a snowflake with the date October 1971. The picture was of the three children in their Halloween costumes, a few days after Ronald's arrival.

The girls had shown very few signs of jealousy when Ronald was adopted. However, Kristen had been so impressed by his blackness that subconsciously, I'm sure, she had insisted on portraying a crow. In the photograph, Ronald and Jessica were framed by Kristen's outstretched black wings. I had made her a pair of bright yellow feet and a beak. Ronald, dressed as Superman, wore a red cape and blue pajamas, with a red S on his chest. Jessica was dressed as an Indian girl, a string of curtain rings about her neck and a feather in a headband.

Numerous ornaments depicted the *three* children.

"Where me?" snapped Hoāng. He grabbed the ornament.

"Hey!" rang out a chorus.

"You pig! You'll break it!" yelled Kristen.

"Mom!" yelled the chorus.

I gently but firmly took the ornament away from him. I had not foreseen all the nonverbal messages Hoāng would be receiving from past Christmases.

"Please, Hoāng Stephen, don't be grabby. Kristen! Don't call him a pig! Come on now, maybe we can find a nice Christmas record."

I led Stephen to the record cabinet. Traditionally, I

had made a family ornament every year. I had yet to make this year's. It would be the first with all six of us in the photograph.

"Okay, kids," called David, clapping his hands. "The lights are on. Now you can put on the ornaments."

I went to the kitchen for the hot chocolate. I could hear the refrain from "Rudolph, the Red-Nosed Reindeer" break out over the speakers. I had forgotten what a terrible record it was! The children's choir was so off-key that I was tempted to grab the record and get rid of it once and for all. I restrained myself because the children seemed to enjoy it. David came in and put his arm around me.

"Relax. Let's have some hot chocolate."

I poured the six cups full and David assembled a tray. When we returned to the living room the stereo was featuring the Chipmunks in "Frosty the Snowman." The children sang along as they hung the ornaments— mostly on the lower branches. I was wincing to the grating quality of the recording when Ronald yelled.

"The cat! The cat got out!"

Just what I did not want to happen! A mad scramble ensued. Jessica scurried under the coffee table after the cat. Popcorn and cranberries flew everywhere!

"The tree! Fluffer Nutter is up the tree!" cried Kristen.

Our peanut-butter-and-white cat was a little over a year old and very frisky. He adored eating tinsel and last Christmas had spent several days running about with a strand or two hanging from his backside.

The cat had been intentionally locked up—we thought! Now ornaments and pine needles were flying everywhere! Hoãng Stephen was at the top of the tree in seconds, grabbing at the terrified cat.

"The tree!" shouted David. He lunged for it, but too

late. Down came tree, lights, ornaments, cat, and Stephen!

My nerves were shot. Never before had Christmas seemed so invaded, so chaotic. Moaning, we picked up the ornaments—some broken, some not. Ronald locked up the cat again. Together we worked to put the tree back to rights. In half an hour we had done the best we could. The tinsel was tangled and draped sideways. The top of a treasured glass star had been broken off. David was clearly exasperated, as he knew I was!

"Let's go, kids. Maybe 'Sesame Street' is on." He herded the children up the stairs.

I turned off the stereo with a shaky hand and collapsed on the couch, feeling numb. Christmas wasn't Christmas. Somehow all the joy, all the shine, all the peace had been stripped away. I rubbed my face, trying to ease the tension.

I stared at the crèche. I had never liked it much; it was cheaply made and the painted faces were crooked. The cardboard stable had dried grass stuck to it. Everything seemed phony. In Joseph's hand was an empty hole where a wire staff once had been held. Made from pressed composition board, the set was mostly brown, brushed with gold paint, now tarnished. Mary's hands and fingers looked like baseball mitts. I looked at the hay in the baby's bed. I looked at the animals—some with worn-down ears; the donkey's foot was missing. Suddenly I was struck by its simplicity; it was what it was. Though cheaply made, it became symbolically beautiful.

I glanced around. The room had all the signs of having been hit by an earthquake. I looked back at the crèche. A baby wrapped in rags, lying in a feeding trough. Poverty! A barn filled with animals—nowhere else to care for a new baby. Rejection! A mother, a father, some farmers and sheep. Surely here was the true meaning of Christmas, here in the rough and rude reality of life.

David came in. He sighed as he sat down beside me. I lifted his arm around me, and he kissed my forehead.

VISIT FROM IMMIGRATION

June 21, 1976

The phone had rung. "Yes, this is Mrs. Purdy. . . . Yes. . . . Hoāng Quan Nguyen, 16 School Street. That's correct." The Department of Immigration wanted to pay us a visit.

Now two days had passed; I waited in the kitchen, trying to keep busy. It was 3:30 P.M. I could see Hoāng Stephen in the driveway on his tricycle.

I hadn't told him too much. What was it the man had said? Civil Liberties was challenging the legality of bringing Vietnamese children to this country. *Now?* After a year had passed and thousands of them were here? *Now* they challenge? No entry cards, no papers—did that make these children less real, less human? Damn! What's legal about war anyway! I scrubbed a pan with a vengeance. Sure, some mothers might have panicked and rushed their children onto planes. But what would there be for Hoāng Stephen if he were returned—half-American and half-Vietnamese in a Communist country? If what the Vietnamese refugees had said about the half-French children were true, Hoāng could be killed if he were to return.

Fingerprints, photos, an interview? What insecurity would such a visit precipitate?

I heard a car pull into the driveway. I drew the curtain aside. A man with glasses was getting out of his car. I went to the front door.

"How do you do, Mrs. Purdy, I'm from the Department of Immigration."

I stepped out defensively onto the porch.

"So this is Hoāng!" he bent down to look into an anxious face. Hoāng's eyes examined the man from head to toe, then fixed on the briefcase.

"Is this going to take long?" I asked.

"No, no, we don't even have to go inside, Mrs. Purdy. I'll set up from my briefcase right here on the porch."

The man opened his brown leather satchel; Hoāng Stephen never left his elbow.

"What's this?" He grabbed a collapsed Polaroid camera.

"It's a camera, son." The officer nervously retrieved his equipment. The case contained all kinds of fingerprinting materials and official looking papers.

"What exactly has to be done?" I asked anxiously.

"It will take only a few minutes," he said, snapping Stephen's picture. "He'll just be photographed, fingerprinted, footprinted, and his United States whereabouts verified. And then I'm off!"

"Yes, but what happens next?"

With a whir . . . r . . . r the photo emerged; Hoāng Stephen's fingers were on it instantly. The man pried the developing image from Hoāng's hand.

"Next? All this information is put on tape, the tape is flown to Saigon and then to trucks that, with the help of loudspeakers, will drive through the streets looking for a mother or parent of these kids."

Left to Right: Ron, Kristen, Jessica, Hoàng Stephen (1975)

"With megaphones? Drive through the streets?" I repeated in disbelief.

"Listen, ma'am, this isn't my idea! Civil Liberties wants these children reclaimed in the event some hasty decisions were made." He opened his ink pad and, one by one, pressed Hoāng Stephen's fingers onto some legal papers. "You'll have to take off your sneakers, son."

"His footprints, too?" My head swam with mixed emotions; it had not been an easy year. Life without Hoāng had been so much simpler. There had been moments when I would have been delighted to see his mother appear! But now—now he surely had become a part of me!

Hoāng sat on the steps, his wrinkled prints, one foot at a time, being pressed on the paper.

"Why his feet?"

"Some babies were footprinted at birth, some handprinted." He shrugged. "Some not at all. It depends on what province he was born in."

"How long could this search take?"

"Oh, maybe a year, Mrs. Purdy. I know this is hard for you."

"Hard? It's hard, all right! If his mother comes forward, then what?"

"The United States has to fly these children back."

If that happens, I thought, it will be the first time our government has come across with a penny for these children.

What kind of goody-goody organization was this, anyway? I turned around to hide my moist eyes. Legalities? Does such a group give one thought to what a return could do to these children; to us, the families?

The officer snapped his briefcase shut. "That's all there is to it, Mrs. Purdy!"

"Good-bye. Say good-bye, Hoāng Stephen." I *hoped*

that was all there was to it! Hoāng waved good-bye and tore down the driveway on his tricycle.

What would I say if I had to tell him he was to be returned? How it would tear my heart out!

I closed the door. Spread before me on the counter were recently developed photos from Flag Day. I picked one up. There was Hoāng Stephen in a Statue of Liberty crown with three big white stars, a construction paper red, white, and blue flag hanging on his shoulders like a sandwich board. In front of his open mouth was a big ice-cream cone. Jessica was in a black leotard, her hair in bunches; Ronald and Kristen in play clothes; grandparents. A picture of the true American family? How many American families were going through this same process? How many had begun building, emotional brick by emotional brick, the foundations of lasting relationships?

CHINESE RESTAURANT

May 19, 1977

Our car pulled up in front of a Chinese restaurant. Two years ago today, we had picked Hoāng Stephen up at the airport. Why was I so intent on celebrating? We pushed through heavy red doors with huge gold Chinese characters.

"I want chopsticks!" shouted Hoāng.

My train of thought was broken, but I soon retrieved it. Hot tea was poured and filled my nostrils. Ahh! The perfect place for Hoāng Stephen! How he adored Oriental food.

"Ron, I know you don't like Chinese food, but there must be something on the menu that appeals to you. It's Stephen's celebration, so do the best you can."

I wondered if my desire for a joyous celebration was my way of placing some positive building blocks in our relationship. Without celebration, we were merely existing, merely coping.

"Be prepared to take some time ordering," I said to David. "You know how many times Stephen changes his mind."

"I know, I know. We'll just order four or five dishes, and we can all share," replied David.

"I don't want to share. I want my own," said Stephen.

"Look, I'm tired of that selfish talk." I grasped him by the chin and looked him in the eye. "Remember the last Chinese restaurant? You were *sure* that what the rest of us had *must* be better than what you had ordered." I could feel my impatience rushing to the fore once again. I was tired of dealing with his predictable disappointments.

"Mom, I have to go to the bathroom." Ronald squirmed, still looking unhappy about the choice of restaurants.

"Me too," said Stephen.

I indicated the restroom sign, which pointed down to the basement.

"Here come the chopsticks!" blurted Jessica.

"I want egg rolls," said Kristen.

The waiter bowed and smiled.

"We'll go ahead and order," said David. "Let's just pick five dishes and get this over with." He looked at me. "I think it actually will be easier for Stephen if *we* do the choosing." We gave the man our order.

"Where *are* those boys, anyway?" I peered over the menu; there was Ronald, rushing toward the table, looking very frightened.

"Mom, Dad, Mom, Dad! There's a man downstairs . . . in the bathroom. . . . He's yelling swears at us!"

"Yelling what?" Instant fright came over me.

"A man. . . . He kept telling us . . . 'Niggers get out. . . . Go home!' I'm scared, Mom. And Stephen's still down there!"

David was on his way down the stairs in a flash. Two boys—ages seven and eight—unsafe in the restroom of a restaurant?

I held Ronald in my arms. The girls leaned into the table, eyes wide and fixed on mine.

"Don't worry, now. Daddy will handle this."

Ronald jumped, hitting my chin with the top of his head. I winced.

"Look! That's the man!" He pointed at a white man seating himself at the next table. I had run into racism before, but this time I was really frightened. We, as protective parents, could not always be with the boys; and as they grew older we would be with them less and less.

Kristen sat upright. "Mom, it's O.K. There's Dad and Stephen!"

The two of them sat down.

"That's the man." Stephen pointed, agreeing with Ronald.

"Don't point!" whispered Kristen.

"Boys," David pressed on in a stern voice, "did either of you say anything to that man? Did he start the conversation?"

"Yes," said Ronald emphatically. "I was coming out of a stall. Stephen was in another one, and this man starts yelling swears at us!"

David looked at me. "As I entered the men's room, he was just coming out."

"Dad," said Stephen, "he kept saying 'shit nigger' . . . then 'Get out of here!'"

Such rotten language assaulting the boys! My heart was racing as I fixed my eyes on the young man and his family. Sandy-haired, in his late twenties, he was the picture of the All-American Boy Scout leader! His lovely wife sat with a toddler in a highchair. An older gentleman sat next to the woman.

"He *must* be spoken to!" I said to David.

"Yes, to be sure. I just have to get the facts."

Our dinner, our celebration, was in ruins. I felt like

throwing up! I abandoned all thoughts but one—David and I, as white parents, if we had any integrity at all, must stand up against this racism!

"Is Dad going to fight him, Mom?" asked Ronald.

"Ron, I'm not going to fight him. But we can't just let this go! That man has to know he can't get away with this! Now, did you boys do or say anything to bother him?"

"He started it," said Ronald. "We were just using the bathroom, and he started swearing at us."

We watched as David got up and approached the young man.

Jessica started to cry. "Is Daddy going to fight the man?"

"Shhh, now, don't cry. Daddy's not going to fight." Rage was choking my throat. I could barely make out what David was saying.

"I'd like to have a word with you." He placed his hand on the back of the young man's chair.

"Who, me?" said the man. "What do you want?"

"Do you see those boys over there?" David was pointing our way. I glared at the man; I felt like a bear protecting its cubs! The young man's face immediately reddened.

"I don't think you'd want me to go into this in front of your family here."

The older gentleman rose to his feet. "What's the problem?"

"I can handle this, Dad." The young man dropped his red napkin on the table. "Really, Dad. I'll just be a minute."

David accompanied the man to the foyer of the restaurant.

"Mom, is Dad going to punch him?" asked Stephen.

"I don't want them to fight!" cried Jessica.

"There isn't going to be a fight," I said. "You kids

have seen too much television." The four children were near tears.

When David returned to the table, he began, "Well, at first he didn't want to admit anything. I told him what you boys said, and he denied it. I told him language like that was not permitted around our house, so I knew you boys were not making it up. Finally I said, 'Is that your young son in the highchair?' He said it was, so I asked him, 'How would like him to be the victim of verbal assaults from some stranger in a men's room, the way you assaulted my sons?'"

"'Hey, look, man!' he said. 'Maybe I did get a little out of hand. I've just had a promotion, and I guess I've had too much to drink. The family and I are just out celebrating. I'm sorry. I really apologize.'"

"Then I said, 'O. K., just don't let it happen again! Picking on little kids is no way to celebrate anything!'"

Our order was assembled before us, but my appetite was shot. The steaming dishes, the bright red napkins spoke of the intended occasion. Merely coping, existing through this meal, was all I could manage.

The ride home was quiet. As we drove along my mind flashed back to our first year in Middleboro. Ronald had been just 5, Jessica, 4, and Kristen, 7.

They were playing in the front yard. At one point I had looked out the window; they were blowing maple seeds like helicopters into the air. Such innocent fun! They would peel the pods apart, stick the winged structures to their noses, make goofy faces, and run about the yard. But soon that glee was shattered. They had come running into the house, terribly frightened by an old man who had "said strange things" to them.

What? What did he say? I wondered.

Jessica asked, "Mom, what's a pet nigger?"

Those three darling faces were all screwed up, their eyes searching mine for answers.

"Mom," said Kristen, "the old man said 'Watcha got there, a pet nigger?'"

"What's a nigger?" asked my adorable Ronald.

"What did he look like?" They described him—an old man, gray beard, bald—a hole in the side of his nose, they said.

There I was, feeling this was too soon to explain what racial hatred was about. There I was, staring into those faces of innocence—Jessica's, still bursting with baby plumpness . . . Kristen's, her fairness flushed from an afternoon of play . . . Ronald's, round and brown, bright and beautiful. There I was, trying to explain why some people have 'a problem'—they believe they are better than others because of the color of their skin.

Later that evening David and I had heard haunting sounds from Ronald's darkened room, muffled at first. But as we stood closer to the slightly open door, we could hear him saying rhythmically as he rocked himself, "Watcha got there, a pet nigger? Watcha got there, a pet nigger?" It was as if the ritual might help him understand, might help him cope with this uneasy intrusion into his world.

Prayers had been said and kisses shared; assuring "I love yous" spoken in our evening ritual with all three children. But as I had thought then, and again as we returned home from the Chinese restaurant . . . when will the slippery snake of racial hatred once more rear its ugly head?

ADOPTION DAY

September 28, 1977

We entered the courthouse in Brockton and worked our way through a sea of people. The day had finally arrived when Hoāng Quan Nguyen legally would become Hoāng Stephen Purdy. Needless to say, I had mixed emotions! From this point on, Hoāng Stephen would be totally our responsibility. I smirked; did legality have anything to do with it? From day one, we had been totally responsible! The years that lay ahead? Obviously, they also would be filled with responsibility.

The corridors of the courthouse seethed with a cross-section of life—lawyers, clients, police, children. A couple argued in one corner; an elderly woman comforted a crying child in another. We were surrounded by human joys and sorrows. In this one building, a person could marry, divorce, adopt, whatever!

Our boys were dressed identically in their maroon and beige shirts, the girls in frilly dresses. David and I had decided to make this day special; we had taken all the children out of school.

"There's Mrs. DePillis!" Ronald smiled and waved.

A pixie of a woman with short graying hair and twinkling eyes made her way toward us.

"It's so good to see you," I said as we embraced.

"Hello, children." She bent down. "Hello, Hoāng."

"Stephen!" he corrected her. Maybe he'll use Hoāng again someday, I thought. Recently he had told a friend he was Puerto Rican. He did not like to be identified with the hordes of impoverished boat people we were seeing daily on television.

"Freda, it's the boys' birthday, remember? I can't believe it's been six years since you called us about Ronald's availability!"

"What do you mean, my availability?" queried Ronald.

"Honey, it was on your third birthday that Mrs. DePillis called to tell us you were 'available' to adopt!"

Last year we had chosen to celebrate the boys' birthdays together, partly because of the timing of Hoāng Stephen's arrival. There was every reason to believe he had never celebrated a birthday, and although his birth card read December 28, we knew he would not understand why Ronald was receiving gifts on September 28, and he was not. The other reason? Kristen's birthday was December 30. Who needed another birthday that close to Christmas!

"Freda, we're having a birthday party for the boys around 3:00; between the two of them, we are expecting about twenty-five children. Is there any chance you can make it?"

"Twenty-five children? I'd love to, but," Mrs. DePillis glanced affectionately at the boys, "I have two other adoptions to process in court today."

Two other adoptions, I thought. I was curious to ask about them, but I knew it was none of my business.

"Mom!" Jessica pulled on my sleeve. "Look!"

Instantly my eyes fixed on Stephen and a police

officer. A holstered gun, hanging from a thick leather belt, was the object of Stephen's curiosity. The officer was startled to feel the small hands clutching.

"Hey, don't touch that!" He bent down from a height of well over six feet.

Ronald shook his head. "I don't believe that kid!"

"Isn't he afraid of anything?" wondered Kristen.

Afraid? I was amazed at what he *was* afraid of, and what he *wasn't!* David was apologizing to the officer.

"Still as precocious as ever!" remarked Mrs. DePillis.

"Honestly, he leaves me speechless!" I replied.

"Reverend and Mrs. Purdy? Mrs. DePillis? The judge will see you now." An efficient-looking woman in a tailored business suit directed us to the judge's chambers.

I held my breath *and* Stephen's hand as we entered the room. The judge, in a regular business suit, sat behind a huge desk. I was disappointed to see he wore no robe.

"Judge, here are the Reverend and Mrs. Purdy and their four children." Mrs. DePillis put her hands on Stephen's shoulders. "This is the young man, Hoāng Quan Nguyen, who will be processed for adoption today."

I was startled to hear his Vietnamese name in full! Until today that really had been his legal name.

"What's this?" asked Stephen as he picked up one object after another from the immense desk. The judge had a collection of every conceivable kind of paperweight. I removed Stephen's hands from a Statue of Liberty and they quickly grabbed a Liberty Bell!

The judge, one eye on Stephen, the other on the papers in front of him, began. "All seems to be in order. If you and Mrs. Purdy will sign here." He pushed the papers across his desk to David, then to me. "Now if my assistant will sign as witness, that's all there is to it!"

"That's it!" I said.

"Easy as one, two, three." The judge smiled.

"Would you mind if I take Stephen's picture with you, Judge?"

"Not at all, but first let me put on my robe!"

He donned his flowing black robe and gestured to Stephen. All smiles, he climbed into the judge's lap.

"Ready?" Easy as one, two, three, I thought.

WHITE PLASTIC SHIELDS

November 10, 1977

Mommy, Mommy . . . Mommy!"

I sat up too quickly; I dangled my feet momentarily until my head seemed to right itself. My digital clock read 4:20 A.M.

"Is that Stephen?" asked David, still buried in his pillow.

"Again." I struggled to my feet. "It's all right; it's my turn. Go back to sleep."

My heart pounded. I groped for my bathrobe. Light from the hall and from Stephen's closet guided me through the darkness.

"Stephen, what is it? I'm here. It's all right. I'm here."

Chubby brown hands grasped me about the neck. Tears and sweaty skin merged with my cheek; his heart pounded. I began to rock him.

"Bad dream! Such a bad dream. A bad man, Mommy!"

"What about a bad man, honey? It was just a dream. Tell me about it. Hush, it was just a dream."

"He was drowning us. Children, many children, all lined up, all walking into deep water."

"Shhh. . . . That's a terrible dream. How frightened you must have been."

A ring of perspiration was visible on the pillow.

Stephen's broken expression was outlined by a contour of light. He looked older when he cried, almost ancient, the imprint of centuries of suffering and oppression etched in his face.

I turned the pillow over. Stephen lay back down.

"A monster. The man was a monster who cast a spell. He had white plastic shields over his eyes, and when he looked at you, you couldn't move. You did what he said. *You* were there, Mom, *you* were there!"

"I was?"

"Yes. I kept asking you, 'Do you love me? Do you love me?'"

My feet were cold. I pulled my nightgown down around them.

"You said, 'yes,' but so softly! And you hardly moved your mouth. You were so far away!"

"Far away? You know I love you. You know that! What a terrible dream."

I hugged and rocked him. I wondered if the nightmares would ever end. During the first few months, the screams were in Vietnamese; after that, clear audible English.

"But there's more, Mom, more." His sobbing had stopped, as if he had made a complete journey from sleep to a conscious reality.

"There were so many children! So many behind me and so many in front of me. There was a tall boy in front of me, and as he entered the water my heart pounded, because I knew I was next! In front of him was a little girl. The monster *had* her, Mommy, but just then the tall boy grabbed her and saved her. Then I woke up."

"Well, thank goodness you woke up!"

Stephen lay back on the pillow. The comic strip characters Snoopy and Lucy encircled his head.

I stroked his curly black hair away from his face. The craggy lines of those ancient times had melted away;

only the scattered pattern of tears remained.

"Now, I want you to promise to call me any time you have a bad dream. I will be here in a moment."

"But, Mom, I'm afraid to go to sleep! I'm afraid I'll have another bad dream!"

"That's why I'm here, honey! Bad dreams are afraid of mommies!"

"But you aren't my first mom, so how can I be a real Purdy?"

"You know, you and I are very much alike. Like you, I'm not a real Purdy either. I was a Chatterton before I married Daddy, so I'm no blood relation to the Purdy side of the family."

Stephen was fully awake, his beautiful brown eyes as large as I'd ever seen them.

"You know it's *love* that makes a real family; we've talked about that many times."

"Mom, can you promise to chase the bad dreams away?"

I cupped my hands on his forehead and shouted into his head. "Bad dreams! Now hear this: This is a mommy speaking, and I command you to leave this minute!"

Stephen was giggling and squirming with delight.

I continued, "This kid here is a real Purdy! Do you hear me? Now leave! Over and out!"

Stephen curled up and rolled over, the light from the closet in his face. The Snoopy pillowcase seemed a bit more appropriate now; even Lucy, in a typical rage, raised her fist above his head as if to echo my command!

PURPLE BUTTER

January 25, 1978

It was unusually quiet in the car. We were returning from sledding with friends and were all pretty tired.

"How was the first animal made?" Stephen's voice broke the silence.

David began with amoebas and was pursuing Darwin's theory of natural selection when Kristen chimed in.

"You see, heredity is passed on through genes established by things like the sun; giraffes' necks are long because over generations of time, their necks needed to stretch to reach the tops of trees." Not bad for a sixth-grader!

"What are genes?" inquired Stephen.

"I'll give you an example," continued Kristen. "Now when Ronald's ancestors lived in Africa, their skin became black because of the heat of the sun—" That was enough! Ronald burst into tears.

"What's wrong?" I asked.

"I don't know. I just don't like talking about this stuff."

I was totally surprised by this outburst. "Ronald, why don't you want to talk about it?" I was feeling terribly judged. Had we not affirmed Ronald's black identity enough over the years?

"It makes me feel as if I'm not a part of this family, as if I don't belong."

"Ronald, Daddy and I have different ancestors. Daddy's came from France and Germany; mine came from England and Ireland." All the while I was speaking in such convincing tones, deep down I was thinking how trite I sounded and how difficult it must be to be black in a white family. Black is such a visible difference. What kind of garbage was I spewing? I loved him so much and wanted him to be happy.

"I forget I'm adopted." Ronald looked at me with tearful eyes. "I forget you didn't born me."

"I'm sorry I didn't born you, honey, but that can't be helped. It does please me that you forgot you were adopted."

We rode along a few minutes more.

"Mom," said Ronald, "if all the butter in the whole world was purple, and you couldn't buy any other color, would you still buy it?"

I reached back and hugged him. "Of course I would."

I was born in vietnam.
Vietnam is a far away contry.
it's a far from here.

I lived in an orphanage
where ther was a lot of kids of kids.
the orphanage was made of brick.

I came here on a jet plane
It took me about 2 or 3 days to get
from vietnam to here but before
I stayin colorado for one month.

It took me six months to
speak the English language

I used to like to go fishing in vietnam
for crabes.
I now have brother and two sisters
and an mother and father that love
me.

DIET FOR HYPERACTIVITY

May 7, 1979

We had moved from Middleboro in 1978. The parsonage here in Winchester was once a carriage barn. I loved its charm and unique look. Sidewalks bordered both sides of the house, sloping down from front to back, so that the full basement was at ground level in the back. It was quite a bird's-eye view from my kitchen window to the street two floors below.

It was 2:30, and I could see the children coming up the walk. Stephen was carrying a crumpled pink tissue.

"Mom, look! My tooth! It came out in school today. There was blood all over the place! Amanda screamed and doesn't want to sit next to me anymore." He carefully unwrapped his treasure. "My teacher says the tooth fairy might come if I put it under my pillow."

"I'll bet she's right. It's worth a try!" Another tooth! At least this one was healthy and due to come out.

Stephen garbled as I looked in his mouth. "I . . . on't . . . hink . . . ere . . . eh . . . a . . . ooth fairy, is there?" I could see the top of a shiny new molar peeking through.

"Why don't you take this upstairs and put it under

your pillow? We'll see in the morning." Before he could run off, I took him by the shoulder for a second look.

"What's that red mark on the bridge of your nose?"

"I don't know. I guess I pinch it sometimes."

"Why do you pinch your nose? You've pinched it so hard you've raised a blood blister there."

"I don't know. I just do."

He was off like a shot, lunchbox tossed clattering onto the kitchen counter. He raced up the stairs.

Only one day on Dr. Feingold's antihyperactivity diet. The regimen had begun yesterday—no salicilates, natural or artificial! There were salicilates in every-thing—oranges, tomatoes, mayonnaise, aspirin. I had spent hours in the store reading labels. How I prayed this would work!

My thoughts were interrupted by Stephen's voice. All I could make out was that something serious had happened to his terrarium. I bounded up the steps two at a time. There was glass all over his bedroom floor.

"How did that break?" There stood the metal frame. Shards of glass, leaves, and dirt were intermingled with his toys.

"I don't know how it broke. I was just tapping the glass to get the cricket down." His eyes registered real disappointment.

"Did you have to tap so hard? You always do everything full force!" I began picking up glass as Stephen lunged for his cricket. "Take that thing outside and let it go."

What had begun as a wonderful experiment, worthy of unlocking the scientist in Stephen, was now literally in pieces. I was so hoping that even one day on that diet would count for something.

6:30 P.M.

"Clear the table, kids. Check the chart to see who loads and who does pans." I needed to talk with David. I had held back all during dinner.

"I really don't know why Stephen's teacher says he's *not* hyperactive. Did you notice that head-jerking during dinner?"

"Yeah, I noticed." David sighed. "He goes from one nervous tic to another."

"Well, I'm afraid he's doubled it this time, between the head-jerking and the nose-pinching." I shook my head.

"At least he's not rolling his eyes back in his head and staring out of the corners anymore!" David mimicked the eye-rolling.

I continued. "Do you see how his head-jerking is synchronized with the word *yes?*" I thought to myself, it's as though he has one extra battery overloading his system. I took a big swallow of hot tea.

David leaned back in his chair and looked at the ceiling. A small grin crept across his face.

"What are you thinking?"

"Oh, I was just wondering if that catsup is still on the ceiling in Middleboro."

I smiled. I had cleaned the nine-foot ceiling of the Middleboro parsonage as best I could. McDonald's catsup packets had been dynamite in Stephen's hands.

"Getting back to the head-jerking," I persisted, "he *is* complaining of terrible headaches."

"It's no wonder! His brain is being banged against the back of his skull all day long! I wonder . . . Stephen!" David called toward the kitchen. "Come here a minute."

"Yep." Stephen arrived, jerking his head in affirmation.

"These headaches you're having. Mommy and I think it's because you're banging and jerking your head all the time."

"Yep," jerked Stephen's head.

"Do you think you could stop doing that? You've gotten into an awful habit!"

"Yep," jerked Stephen's head.

David reached into his pocket. "Here's a dime." He placed it on the table. "I want you to sit here for a full five minutes and see if you can stop jerking your head. Then you can have the dime."

"Yep," jerked Stephen's head. He caught himelf and grabbed the sides of his head in disappointment. The other children wandered in and quickly caught on to the contest.

"Can we start again?" He grinned. "I wasn't ready."

"You tell me when you're ready. But two things—no, three things—you can't hold your head, it has to be a full five minutes, *and* you have to talk to me."

Stephen stiffened up and sat like stone. I could see his eyes fixed on that dime! Somehow, I knew psychiatry would think this procedure horrendous! On the other hand, from what we had learned about behavior modification, there certainly was a goal and a reward!

David began. "What did you bring home from school today?"

"I lost a tooth in school." Stephen talked like a robot, body stiff, lips tight.

"Did you put it under your pillow?"

"Yep," jerked Stephen's head.

"You can't do it," laughed Kristen.

"You lose!" laughed Ron and Jessica.

"Don't tease," I interrupted. "Stephen can't help it; it's a terrible habit."

116

"Here's the dime anyway." David patted him on the shoulder. "Try not to jerk your head anymore, O.K.?"

I looked at David. Not two minutes had passed!

"Upstairs now, all of you. You must have homework." I couldn't help wondering whether the Feingold Diet would really work. Was it eliminating certain foods that helped, or was it merely the extra attention supplied by the diet?

9:00 P.M.

"Who's up?" I could hear shuffling in the hall.

"I am. I can't sleep." Stephen wandered into my room. "The tooth fairy isn't coming. There *is* no tooth fairy." He flopped on my bed.

"But honey, it's not morning yet. Give the fairy some time."

"I threw it away."

"You what?"

"I threw away my tooth. It's in the wastebasket."

"Stephen, isn't it worth the chance that the tooth fairy might come?" I stared at him in disbelief. Is this what deprivation does to a child? Is he more comfortable living with disappointment? Is there no hope left inside his being?

"Come on now, back to bed." I was determined to get a quarter under his pillow whether he was asleep or not.

"I'll go down and get you a glass of juice. That will help you sleep." As soon as he was tucked in, I headed downstairs, grabbed a quarter and a glass of apple juice, and returned.

"Here's your juice. Now, where is that tooth?" I began poking in the wastebasket, found it, and slipped it into my pocket. "Not here. The tooth fairy must have found it."

Stephen jumped out of bed and began pawing through the basket. I quickly moved over to his bed and slid the quarter beneath the pillow.

"Maybe there's a quarter here somewhere, honey. You know it's a good sign when there's no tooth around." I pulled back the covers. Stephen ran to the bed and flung his pillow aside.

"A quarter. The fairy left a quarter!" Holding the coin by its edge in his two hands, he flopped on the bed and rolled over on his back to admire his trophy.

"Mom, you put it there, didn't you?" He grinned from ear to ear.

"Me? What? Who, me?" I exclaimed in mock seriousness, hands over my heart. I hugged him. "Now maybe you can get some sleep. Goodnight."

I kissed his forehead and left the room. I thought I needed to move back in my mind to ground zero to understand this child. Maybe if I eliminated any childhood pleasure from my own memory, experienced repeated disappointment. Then maybe I could understand the inner workings of his head!

May 18

After ten days of Dr. Feingold's diet I gave up. I saw no change in Stephen's behavior. Reports from school were very discouraging. He was not retaining what he learned and doing very poorly in math, which used to be his strength. I decided to bombard him with salicilates for two days to see if he'd become *more* hyperactive. No change! Many times I had seen him with gum or candy that another child had given him. To really test that diet with Stephen, I'd have to lock him in a cell and pass his food under the door.

REAL MOTHER

June 18, 1979

The boys shared the huge master bedroom of the parsonage in Winchester. Kristen, our oldest, now in junior high, left for school a full hour earlier than Jessica; since the boys' schedules were alike, we had decided to try putting them together again.

To give as much privacy as possible, we placed a long folding screen down the middle of the room, using desks and bureaus, back to back, to hold it up. There were identical walk-in closets at each end of the room.

Stephen liked to play in his closet. He used the metal frame of a butterfly chair and blankets to build a fort. He also liked to sleep in his closet. He had slept on a straw mat in Vietnam, so he must have felt more secure on the floor in his sleeping bag.

We had assumed the need would wear off in time, but it was now three months since he had begun to squirrel himself away at bedtime. We had struggled with our feeling that it was not right for our child to be sleeping in a closet. But the fact that the nightmares were far less frequent gave us some reassurance that it was helpful.

Our decision to move to Winchester had been made partly because of Stephen. David had accepted the appointment in the Boston area since we felt professional help was necessary. And although we discovered that most professionals seemed to think *we* were the only therapy Stephen needed, we had placed him with a play therapist one hour a week, and David and I saw an associate once a month. We were forced to discontinue therapy after a year and a half, however; our insurance didn't begin to cover all the costs, and we had run out of savings.

8:00 P.M.

It was Monday night, and I was making rounds, saying goodnight. The light from Stephen's closet was streaming across the room. I could see him inside.

"Stephen, honey, are you ready for bed?"

"No." He sat crosslegged on his sleeping bag, looking at a book in his lap.

"Why, what's the matter? . . . What are you reading?"

"Mom, why did you save all these clippings?" He was leafing through his baby book.

"Clippings? . . . Those clippings are about you. . . . Don't you know how special you are?"

"Ronald's picture wasn't in the paper, was it?"

"No, now that I think about it. No . . . I guess not." I continued, "I guess your adoption had more to do with politics than Ron's did."

"What's politics, anyway?"

"That's a good question, honey." I knelt and sat on one corner of his sleeping bag. "I would say . . . because this country was committed to winning a war in Vietnam for so long, there was, and still is, more interest in your adoption."

"Yeah. But these clippings, now that I can read. . . . It's so hard . . . reading about myself."

120

Hoang loved his closet.........

Pamela Chatterton Purdy 1981

"What part is hard, honey?"

"Like this—'Orphan Finds Good Home. . . . Hoāng is a good-looking male child of five.' . . . I can hardly remember my first mother."

Stephen picked at a corner of the book and a few tears rolled down his face. My eyes felt moist.

"I'm so sorry this upsets you. . . . And I'm sorry you can hardly remember your first mother."

His lower lip quivered. He went on, "How can I love you so much when you're not my real mother?"

My own tears welled up; I kissed his forehead and stroked his hair. I was deeply touched and waited a moment until my voice returned.

"That's both sad and wonderful. . . . I'm overwhelmed by what you say."

"Mom . . . if my real father was a black American soldier, and my real mother was Vietnamese, how could they get together, if they were fighting on different sides?"

"Do you know what a civil war is, honey? It's a war when one part of a country fights another part. It was the South Vietnamese against the North Vietnamese. Your father was in Vietnam because the United States decided to take sides with the South. Your mother lived in South Vietnam, so your mother and father were on the same side. The North finally took over the South, and that's why your mother, along with other mothers of half-American children, decided you would be safer in this country. During the last year of the war, many of you were put into orphanages, hoping to get you to safety."

Stephen slid his pencil back and forth in his slipper sock, then lay on his back.

"Why do I have to look different? Why can't I look like everyone else?"

"Jessica and Kristen look different, and they're

biological sisters. I have a twin, and she and I look different. Ronald is different."

"I know. . . . I know, it's just that it would be fun to have straight blond hair—you know, the way Billy's hair is. It hangs in his eyes and it's so cool the way he flips it back."

I lay on my back beside him, covering my eyes from the bright light. It really was secure and cozy here on the floor, every nook and cranny visible. Besides a clock, a tissue box, and a radio, Stephen had pictures of beautiful birds taped all over the walls. He had torn them from *Ranger Rick* magazines.

"You know, these pictures add a lot to your closet. What if all these birds looked alike? What then?"

"The world would be dull."

"Sure would. . . . You know God made us all different, and the world is a more beautiful place because of it."

"Mom, I guess what I'm saying is that I hate being called Blackie and Cotton Picker at school. I wish I were white."

I propped myself up on one elbow. "Being called names has nothing to do with who you really are. . . . Kids who call names have a problem; someone who has to put someone else down has a problem!"

I gathered him in my arms. It made me cry, too, that there was such cruelty at school.

"I love you, Mom. . . . How can that be, when you're not my real mother?"

"Hey, I love you and you love me. . . . What else do we need, to be a real mother and son?"

I glanced at the clock propped up on two cloth-covered bricks—9:30. The big house with its many rooms was dark and quiet.

CLOSET CONVERSATION WITH DAVID

July 28, 1979

K risten, Ronald, and I were staying at my mother's house, just down the street from our summer cottage. Our stay on the Cape was officially over and our house was rented to others now, but since Ronald and Kristen had been cast in *The Hobbit*, I was staying with them for the additional performances. Ronald had the lead as King Thorn, and Kristen was an elfin guard. Jessica and Stephen had returned to Winchester with David.

The phone rang in the kitchen darkness.

"David! I'm so glad you called." I settled into a chair. "I miss you."

"I miss you, too, honey."

"How are Jessica and Stephen?"

"Fine." David chuckled.

"What's funny?"

"Oh . . . would you believe your son is now back in his closet in all this heat?"

"What? He hasn't been in that closet for a month."

"Well, he's re-ensconced. I went into his room last night to kiss him goodnight, and there he was. That closet is set up like a miniature house! I crawled in beside him. He was delighted and showed me all the

features. Now he's even rigged up a string from his light switch so it dangles down where he can reach it."

I laughed. "I can see you now. How could you stand the heat?"

"It wasn't that bad. Anyway, he told me how happy he was that I was there with him, how much he loved us, you and me. He said he didn't like it when we were angry with him, that it upset him when you and I argued."

"Argued? We hardly ever do."

"I know. He said he worries that we might get a divorce. Then he wouldn't know who he would live with. He was really sweet. He said since he loved us both he wouldn't be able to choose between us. I told him that just because we occasionally argue doesn't mean we'd be divorced. People can disagree, argue, even fight, and still love each other. He was relieved to hear that."

"Oh, honey, I'm so glad you had a chance for that time together."

"Well, toward the end of our talk, he said he was so happy that even when he was scolded, he would remember our little talk. I can't word it exactly as he said it—something to the effect that the deep love he felt between us would help him not to be so afraid when we were angry with him. He would remember that he was loved. He's really very reflective."

I sighed a huge sigh. "Yes, he is. And thank goodness he shares that side of himself. It really makes the rough spots more bearable."

SCAPEGOATING

October 14, 1979

I t was 2:30 and David had just finished a late lunch. He kissed me good-bye and said he was off to the hospital to visit a parishioner. The phone rang.

"Mom?" It was Jessica. She was crying. "They're killing Stephen! They're beating him! I'm scared!"

"Who's beating Stephen? Who?"

"A whole bunch of kids. They're out on the playground." Her voice was trembling.

"Isn't there a teacher on duty?" I signaled David to wait.

"No. Well, the bell has rung and I guess they are all on their way home. Come quickly, please! They're killing him!"

"One of us will be right down." I hung up and stared at David.

"The school playground; a whole bunch of kids are beating Stephen! Can you go?" The school playground was just two blocks down the street.

"On my way." David shook his head in disbelief as he hurried out.

I thought yet again of the untallied hours spent trying

to untangle Stephen's life. Off David had gone, in suit and tie, to break up a fifth-grade fight.

A half-hour later David, Stephen, and Jessica came through the kitchen door. David's shirt was unbuttoned and his tie was loose. Hands on hips, he spoke.

"Stephen, I want you in my office. You, Mom, and I are going to have a little talk."

Stephen's shirt was torn. He was covered with dirt. He stole a quick glance at my unhappy face as he walked past. Jessica ran to me. How upset she was! I hugged her, marveling at her sensitivity and love for her brother.

"What happened?" I asked David. "What in the world was going on?"

"Well, when I got there, all I could see was a pile of kids and fists flying. So I grabbed one at a time and peeled them off until I got to the bottom. Seems Stephen had been taunting some child about his drunken father, and that's how it all started. Stephen's teacher happened along, so we had a little talk."

"Stephen was teasing a kid about his drunken father? But what about all the other kids who were fighting?"

"The teacher says Stephen has a sixth sense—the kid's father *is* an alcoholic. Stephen has insulted so many children over the past few months that once he was down, *all* the kids beat on him."

"What are we going to do with him? Do you think this is what the doctor referred to as *scapegoating?*"

"Sure I do. The psychiatrist is absolutely right. Stephen has such a negative self-image that he sets himself up. He thinks he's nothing inside; therefore he sets out to tear others down. The teacher used the term *Achilles heel*. He says Stephen is so perceptive he knows exactly where another child's Achilles heel is." David stared out the kitchen window. "He seems to want the other children to feel as lousy as he does. He sets up a situation to prove to himself that he's no good.''

David slowly turned and headed toward his office. As I followed, myriad thoughts flashed through my mind. It had been four years since we had picked Stephen up at Logan. Are the first five years of a child's life so formative that his attitude about himself is unchangeable?

BOAT PEOPLE

December 26, 1979

Light penetrated my heavy sleep. Lying comfortably on my back, I became aware of my deep breathing as black and white images prodded my eyes. Squinting, I swam through swells of surf; foamy brine heaved me up, dropped me, washed me left, twisted me right. Sitting up, I could barely make out an object. It came into focus, then disappeared. A boat, sails torn, bobbed to the surface, sank. Human forms, huddled together, some hanging on, some waving for help. I reached to turn up the volume.

"These people sometimes search in vain for a port of entry. Adrift for weeks at a time, boat people are often victims of piracy and rape, starvation and drowning."

How incredible to sit here in warmth and comfort. The broadcast continued. "Refugees by the thousands are fleeing Vietnam and Cambodia . . . "

"Mom, are those people going to make it to shore?" Jessica's voice interrupted the commentator. I was startled. I had not noticed her enter the room. I pulled her down beside me.

"I don't know, honey. I hope so. Sometimes I think

we are living in the only warm, well-fed corner of the earth."

We talked, but our eyes remained riveted to the TV—such pathetic, desperate souls.

"Mom, why doesn't someone help them?"

Now ten years old, Jessica was as sensitive and compassionate as ever.

"Some people *are* helping them, honey. Some of them, anyway. Did you know that a refugee family moved to Winchester just last week? Two of the children will be attending your school."

"Oh, I think I saw them. Last week I was in the lunchroom when the principal came in with some children that looked Vietnamese. You mean they came over on a boat, like these people on TV?"

"Yes, and from what the newspaper says, they have been through a horrible ordeal."

"But how did they get from there to here?"

"Well, I honestly don't know all the details, but I do know that the Ecumenical Association here in Winchester sponsored them. I mean they have found them a house, and they will pay the rent for a while and hope to find jobs for the parents and a nephew. They live right around the corner on Wildwood Street. We really must have the whole family here for dinner soon."

The news quickly focused on another part of the world; then another; then a few commercials. How indiscriminate this thing called television, with its ability to pick and choose, cause concern and compassion, depict hunger and disease—all in the comfort of one's living room.

I was sure of one thing—the images of those boat people had me wide awake and overcome with concern.

December 27

"Here's the basket of fruit, Stephen. Wear your gloves; it's very cold and we are going to walk."

I handed David the Vietnamese/English dictionary, grabbed the calendar off the kitchen wall, and we were on our way.

"Why aren't the rest of the kids coming?" said Stephen.

"Because," David explained, "we don't want to overwhelm them. They speak no English, and it's going to be confusing enough to try to understand one another. Somehow, we'll attempt to invite them to dinner."

We turned onto Wildwood Street. Stephen was a gush of nonstop questions.

"Mom, don't tell them I'm Vietnamese."

"Oh! You don't think they are going to figure that out?"

"Yeah, but I'm an American now."

"Stephen, don't you think they would be interested to know they are not the only Vietnamese in Winchester?" said David.

"I'd like to introduce you by your first name—Hoāng," I suggested. "It may be the only word they understand—that's if we're pronouncing it right."

The cold, crisp air added to my excitement. How wonderful to have this family living just around the corner from us here in predominantly white Winchester. The paper had indicated that one child would be a fifth-grader, along with Jessica and Stephen.

The small house was painted a picturesque Wedgewood blue with white trim. A farmer's porch ran across the entire front. We mounted the steps and rang the doorbell. A small child opened the door wide, and in an instant, all seven members of the family were on their feet, bowing, talking, gesturing for us to come in.

"Welcome to Winchester," said David. We bowed awkwardly, talked, smiled, and shook hands.

Thanh, the twelve-year-old boy, smiled at Stephen as if he recognized him from school. Thanh had the same dental problem as Stephen, but was lighter skinned, thinner, and taller. His hair was shiny and straight, and his brown eyes reflected no upper lid, the way Stephen's did. Moreover, Thanh exhibited a calm, a sense of security I had never seen in Hoāng Stephen.

I allowed my eyes to fully absorb the beauty of the delicate Oriental faces. I had not expected the children to look so different from our Stephen. I had tried to memorize the names I had read in the newspaper, though I knew my pronunciation would probably be way off. The three girls, ranging in age from six to eighteen, looked very much alike—delicate, shy, and oh, so thin.

"Seet . . . down . . . please," gestured a young man. I guessed him to be Hien, the nephew. I had read much about the family.

"This is our son, Hoāng Stephen," I said. More bowing.

Stephen gave Mrs. Tran the basket of fruit. Tiny and shy, she took the gift with one hand, smiled, and patted Stephen's head with the other.

"We"—David pressed his hands to his chest—"would like to invite you"—he opened his palms to the family—"to dinner."

Thank goodness Hien speaks some English, I thought.

Blank stares darted around the room, followed by streams of sing-song Vietnamese.

"Eat," said Stephen, cupping one hand and scooping the other toward his mouth.

"Oh." Mrs. Tran nodded, jumped up, and went into

the kitchen. I wondered if Stephen could understand any of this.

"Sone . . . tea?" asked Hien.

"No," said David. "I mean yes." He grabbed the dictionary. He was thinking exactly what I was thinking. We did not want to insult them by not having tea. Yet how were we going to make it clear that we wanted *them* to have dinner with *us*? This was not going to be easy.

"Here." David showed Hien the dictionary. "Dinner . . . you . . . family . . . have dinner with us."

"Din . . . ner?"

David quickly showed him the calendar. "December 31—5:00." He pointed to the five on his watch.

"Ah, yes." Hien continued in Vietnamese to his family, then went into the other room and returned with his own calendar.

The air was pungent with the smell of cooking oil. The thermostat must have been set at eighty degrees; I could tell that this family was in for a big adjustment to our New England climate!

Mrs. Tran returned with a tray of hot tea. More talk in Vietnamese continued.

"Yes, yes. . . . Thang . . . you. . . . Sone tea, please?" bowed Hien.

"Thank you, yes," we all nodded.

"Hoāng Stephen , do you understand anything they are saying?"

"No. I only remember a few words, like dooie . . . banana."

"Ah," nodded the family, smiling and pointing toward the bananas in the basket of fruit.

Hien began speaking to Hoāng Stephen in Vietnamese. Stephen shook his head.

"I don't understand. . . . Not anymore." He looked

at me, his face screwed up in disbelief. "How did I ever talk like that?"

"Well, it has been more than four years, honey."

My mind raced ahead. How would we ever make it through an entire evening with this family? Would it be filled with dead spaces of silence, much bowing and well-intended smiles?

Hien marked his calendar and nodded.

"We"—David pressed his fingers to his chest—"will pick you up . . . ah . . . " He started to point out the window at our car, then remembered we had walked. He thumped the calendar with his finger. "December 31—5:00."

December 31

5:00 P.M.

"They're here, they're here!" squealed Jessica. All four children ran to the window.

I opened the front door. On the hall table I had placed name tags for our visitors.

"Kids, are you all wearing your name tags?"

"Yes," rang out a chorus. The Tran family came up the walk, the smaller children huddled close to their mother.

"Mrs. Tran, Mr. Tran, welcome, welcome! Hello, children."

Mrs. Tran handed me a dish containing a strange gelatinous substance. It was a clear brown, with some kind of foamy, bubbly topping.

"Thank you. How nice of you." I bowed.

"Let me take your coats. Children, help Thanh, Le Quyen, and Le Quan," I said, reading the name tags.

David helped Hien with his coat. I was shocked—it had to be a boy's size, maybe a twelve. A full five inches of his wrists were showing.

Kristen, Stephen, and I carried the coats—some too big, some too small—into David's study.

As I placed a name tag on each of the Trans, I tried to pronounce their names. Hien smiled sweetly and repronounced them with me.

I had built a roaring fire in the fireplace and had remembered to turn up the thermostat.

David took off his jacket and looked at me. "Isn't it a little warm in here?"

"Just for tonight, honey." I turned to the Tran family. "Sit down, won't you?" I gestured to the couch and chairs. On the coffee table I had placed the children's baby books, along with other photo albums.

"Hoãng Stephen," David began, "show the Trans the pictures of you when you first came to live with us."

"Girls, why don't you take Le Quan and Le Quyen upstairs and show them your dollhouse." Jessica and Kristen stood up.

"Dollhouse . . . upstairs." Kristen gestured.

"Toy house, little house." Jessica mimed smallness with her hands.

The Vietnamese girls clung more tightly to their mother. Jessica and Kristen glared at me in embarrassment. Oh well, so much for that idea.

Stephen had seated himself next to Hien and was studying his face carefully. Although the newspaper had said the young man was only twenty-one, he seemed older. They looked at the photos together. Much sing-song Vietnamese and head nodding accompanied each photo. Hien repeatedly patted Stephen on the shoulder.

Stephen got up for a moment to whisper in my ear. "Mom, I think he wants to be my father."

"Isn't that nice, dear?" I forced a smile to hide my fear that this might actually be a desire on Stephen's part.

"Stephen, why don't you show the children that

game you learned in Vietnam? You know, the one where you thump your knuckles and bang your elbow? These children might know the game."

"Oh, I don't want to."

"Come on, Stephen, go ahead!" chimed in our other kids.

Stephen grinned and placed his arm on the table, palm up. Arching his wrist, he began thumping his knuckles from little finger to index finger, as if in a drum roll; then he banged his elbow—tap, tap:

Br . . . r . . . rump, tap, tap,

Br . . . r . . . rump, tap, tap,

Br . . . rump, Br . . . rump, Br . . . rump, tap, tap.

It had a military ring and was done rapidly, with such precision—each knuckle hit separately. The other children could only come close to such a sound.

The Vietnamese children watched with blank expressions, then shook their heads. Another futile attempt!

"Well, dinner's ready. Excuse me a minute." I began bringing the food to the dining room table. The table would not seat thirteen, so we served buffet style.

David clapped his hands. "Kids, go help Mom."

From early morning the children and I had chopped, cooked, stirred, then chopped some more. I had used an Old World cookbook, coming as close to some Indonesian recipes as possible. There were oohs and ahhs as we encouraged our guests to fill their plates.

Mrs. Tran and the oldest daughter held back. I was last in line, and it took much coaxing to get them to take even a little.

Then I remembered what I had read in my cookbook. The book was old, so I wasn't sure whether the customs it mentioned were still practiced. According to my book, Indonesian and Cambodian women first served their families and ate only after the others had finished.

We took our plates to the living room. The Vietnamese children ate as if they were really hungry. Occasionally they were admonished by their mother; then they would glance around and eat more slowly.

I never saw Mrs. Tran or her oldest daughter take a bite, although the food disappeared from their plates. I noticed they looked so uncomfortable.

"Mom, this is really good." Stephen sat down with a second heaping plateful.

"Come, children, help yourselves to more," I encouraged the Tran children. They did not need much urging.

"Hien . . . you and family . . . come here . . . on boat," said David.

"Boat?" questioned Hien. David reached for the dictionary.

"Oh . . . boat! Yes, we come . . . here . . . lon time. . . . Take . . . lon time."

"The paper said your boat landed in Malaysia." David spoke slowly, enunciating every word.

"Malaysia. . . . Yes. . . . Malaysia. . . . But . . . how you say . . . shoot. . . . People shoot at us. . . . Try . . . make us away."

"They shot guns at you?"

Hien smiled at Ronald, not understanding what he had said.

"How many people were on your boat?" I spoke slowly.

"How . . . many?" Hien reached for a pencil, then spoke in Vietnamese as he wrote 157. "Very small boat. . . . Many die." He flipped through the dictionary and pointed to the word *factory*.

"Fac . . . tory. . . . We put in factory, locked in." He flipped more pages.

He pointed. "Rice. We ate . . . one cup rice . . . five day. Later . . . we wait ten day."

"Each of you had one cup of rice every five to ten days?" I shook my head. Hien smiled, and I could tell he had understood some of what I said.

"Yes. . . . We . . . so . . . hungry." He searched further in the dictionary, but evidently could not find the right word.

"We . . . make hole . . . how you say . . . fence. Then . . . police beat us."

"That's terrible." Kristen, with her red hair and fair skin, stood out in this group.

"So . . . we . . . back on boat . . . many day. . . . But . . . we here now." Hien placed his hand on his chest. "We here. . . . America . . . the best."

Then he spoke in Vietnamese and the whole family repeated, "Yes. . . . America . . . best."

"Let's have some dessert, kids." The children followed me into the kitchen. A friend from the Ecumenical Association had mentioned that Mrs. Tran's birthday was January 1. We had pointed out birthdays and birthday cakes in family photographs earlier in the evening, careful to hold up the right number of fingers for the ages. Not sure whether I would embarrass Mrs. Tran, I lit the candles, and we all sang as I placed the cake before her. Her face glowed in the candlelight—Old World and New World coming together—despite the creases of despair, she looked beautiful. We showed her the word for *birthday* in the dictionary.

"Ah . . . " She put her hands to her face. Tears welled up in her eyes.

Hien spoke to her at length in Vietnamese.

"Now blow out the candles," said Stephen.

"I don't think she understands," I said. "Why don't you children blow them out?"

Everyone looked delighted at this strange custom. I began to cut the cake.

"Now." Mrs. Tran held up one finger and went to get her dish.

"Eat . . . now," said Hien.

Mrs. Tran cut the harder-than-gelatin mixture into squares, and we placed cake and squares together on the plates.

Ronald looked as if he'd rather die than eat the wiggly stuff. I took a courageous bite, determined to love it.

"It's good, children!"

Mrs. Tran beamed. It was sweet and actually very good. Hoāng Stephen bolted his down and looked for more.

We spent the rest of the evening watching home movies—the boys arriving by plane, the children in the snow. There was much laughter over those of the children ice-skating. Hoāng Stephen was always over on his ankles. Each time a child fell there were gales of laughter. David would then reverse the film, causing the children to return quickly to their feet. Thank God for pictures worth a thousand words!

David turned on a living room light. "Honey, didn't your dad bring us a big box of ice skates last year?"

"Yes, he did, and I'm sure we have enough."

The evening ended in the front hall around a box of skates, where we managed to fit all the Tran children. They were so excited. There was a pond, frozen solid at the moment, within walking distance of their house. We also managed to fit Hien with one of David's old coats. It had been a good evening.

January 10, 1980

The phone rang. It was the school nurse. Le Quan, the youngest of the Tran children, was sick; only six years old, she had active tuberculosis. There was evidence of open lesions on her tiny lungs. We and others who had been in contact with her family were being advised to have TB tests.

I slowly hung up the phone. It was a wonder their whole family didn't have TB—adrift for months in a boat half full of water, and now living in a freezing New England climate!

I was not afraid any of us had contracted the disease. I had no intention of having us tested. If to love is to risk, I was glad we had risked.

HALF-PINT NIGGER

June 17, 1981

I was enjoying a hot shower when a fist pounded on the door.

"Mrs. Purdy, Mrs. Purdy, come quick! Ronald told me to come get you!"

I turned off the shower. I wasn't sure what I had heard! Dripping wet, I shouted, "Jason? Is that you? What is it? What's the matter?"

"Stephen's been hit! Come quick!"

"Hit? What do you mean, hit?" The hot water turned to ice on my skin. I grabbed for a towel and opened the door a crack. Jason Boyd, a neighbor, Ronald's friend, was running back downstairs, screaming, "Hurry, come quick!"

I grabbed my nightgown, threw it on, and tore down the steps.

A towel to stop the bleeding, I thought as I sped through the kitchen. Barefoot, I ran outside. The pavement was rough; my hair was dripping down my neck; the red nightgown stuck to me as I ran. I could see Stephen stumbling up the street. He was holding his head with both hands.

Hit by a car? Oh, my God! Has he been hit by a car? His face was contorted in pain; tears mingled with blood; his mouth was open wide, twisted down at the corners. It seemed he could hardly breathe. His eyes were swollen shut with tears.

I had seen pictures of the war. Vietnamese children—naked screaming children—running in the streets, vaseline-thick napalm burning their skin. All of America had seen these pictures; now I was seeing reality!

Wilma, Jason's mother, was running toward Stephen with a towel as I ran toward him with mine.

"My God, Stephen, what happened? What happened?" I wrapped my towel around his head; Wilma wiped his face with hers.

"He hit me—some guy! At the corner store." Between gulps of air, he continued. "He grabbed me by the throat and choked me. His arms—his arms were all muscles with veins sticking out."

"A man did this to you? A person hit you like this?"

Rage welled up in me, an anger that shattered me in a way I had never known before. Another human being had done this deliberately?

I had always prided myself on my strength during an emergency. As the mother of four I had seen cuts, the need for stitches, twisted knees, and I had always been able to react responsibly and drive calmly to the emergency room. Now as I thanked Wilma and started toward the house, I began to shake all over. With each step, I felt my legs tremble.

"Come inside." My arm around Stephen, I pressed the towel against his head. Both his elbows were dripping blood. A pool had stained his white shirt as it ran down and collected in the hollow of his neck.

I held his head over the sink and carefully poured cold water through his blood-soaked hair. Bloody water swirled into and over the lunch dishes. Black curls swished aside, revealing an ugly laceration. Stephen cried softly as I toweled and examined his head.

"Why did he do this? Did you know him? How did this happen?"

"I don't know. I never saw him before. He kept hitting my head on the Coke machine."

"The Coke machine! Come lie down on the couch." The bleeding seemed to be under control.

"The police! I'm going to call the police." My hands would not stop shaking.

"The police? What for? Are you going to report him?"

"Of course I am! I'm furious! I can't believe someone would beat up a sixth-grade kid like this." I looked for a pencil. I was so shaken I knew I had to write it all down before I made the call.

Jason and Ronald came through the kitchen door.

"Tell me, Stephen! Exactly what happened? Now, from the beginning. Can you describe him?"

I sat with paper and pencil and tried to collect myself. My writing was horrendous!

"I was walking downtown to buy a squirt gun and a Father's Day card when this guy tried to run me over."

"Run you over? With his car? Can you describe the car?"

"It looked like the green one we used to have."

"Ron, get a paper and pencil and put it in your pocket. I want you boys to walk downtown. *Do not open your mouths!* If you see a car of that description, I want you to write down the license number. Honey, think now. What did the man look like?"

"He was tall. He had dark brown hair and heavy eyebrows and no shirt on."

"Got that, Ron? But remember, not a word! And don't let anyone see you writing down a license number."

The boys set out on their mission.

I took another look at Stephen's head. The swelling under the laceration was considerable, but the bleeding still seemed under control.

"Was there anyone in the store who watched what was going on?"

"Yes, Mom. There must have been six or seven people standing in line."

"And no one helped you or tried to stop this bully?"

"No, Mom, they all just watched!"

"Just watched a sixth-grader being beaten? I can't believe this! Did anyone offer you help, once you were left lying there?"

"No, no one said anything. Oh yeah. A man looked down at me and said, 'You probably deserved it.'"

You probably deserved it! Why? I thought. What possible reason could there be to justify the choking and beating of an eleven-year-old boy? Racism, that's all it was!

"Before I call the police, is there anything else this bully said to you?"

"Yeah, he swore a lot. He told me to get out of the road."

"Out of the road? What road? What happened?"

"When I was crossing the intersection—that's when he first saw me. He wasn't going to stop. I had to jump out of his way."

"Jump out of his way?"

"Yeah, he gunned for me."

"Then what happened?"

"A lady—she was walking in front of me. She said, 'Stay away from that guy. He's trouble.' And I said, 'Yeah, he's a jerk!'"

"You called him a jerk?"

"Yeah, Mom—he almost ran over me! Anyway, he must have heard me, 'cause he parked across the street and started yelling swears at me. Then I went into the store and he came in and grabbed me."

"When he grabbed you, did you smell alcohol, beer? What did he say?"

"I didn't smell anything. Oh, yeah, he called me a half-pint nigger!"

"A half-pint nigger! Oh, my God, and I just sent your brother off to look for this lunatic!"

I felt total panic. My nerve endings seemed to fly off in all directions. I started for the door—no. I turned to the phone. I thought of Jason. I had sent him off with Ron. Surely a twisted mind would see him as a white "nigger lover."

The kitchen clock said 3:15. I dialed 411—no, dummy, that's information—I dialed again.

"I want to report an assault. My son was just assaulted downtown." The words were mine, but they sounded so impossible!

"Just a moment, ma'am. What's your name and address?"

"Of course, yes. That's Pamela Purdy, 16 School— no, 30 Dix Street." I couldn't believe I had started to give our old address!

"Go ahead, ma'm. You say your son was assaulted?"

"That's right. My eleven-year-old son was in the store when a total stranger walked in, picked him up by the throat—off the floor—swore at him, called him a half-pint nigger, and bashed his head against a Coke machine." My voice was a wreck!

"Can you describe this person, Mrs. Purdy, and give us the location of the attack?"

"Yes." I gave the lieutenant the details and described the man and his car.

"Stephen, how old do you think this man was?" I asked, my hand muffling the phone.

"Oh, a big kid—maybe high school."

"A big kid—maybe high school—my son says."

"O.K., ma'am, we'll look for him."

I hung up and ran upstairs to dress. I caught my reflection in the hall mirror. I looked dreadful!

What did the officer just say—"We'll look for him"? Don't they want to send someone over to question Stephen?

I threw on a blouse and wraparound skirt. I wished David were home. I went back downstairs. Stephen was still lying on the couch, holding his head. I switched on the TV for him.

"Stephen, I'm going out to look for your brother and Jason. When I get back, I'm going to take you to the hospital."

"Hospital? Hospital?"

"Don't worry. I just want to make sure you're all right. And unless a doctor checks you over, it's just that kid's word against ours." I knew a record of the injury must be recorded by a physician.

I threw down my hairbrush and ran out the door. Should I walk or drive? I jumped into the car. No sign of the boys. I drove on. Where were they?

I turned down another street. The corner store came into view. A space was available almost in front. With a feeling of clear purpose, I parked, my eyes fixed on the shop. I felt a sudden strength as I opened the door and marched up to the man at the counter. He was leaning on one elbow, working a crossword puzzle.

I tapped my car keys on the counter. "I want to know what went on here this afternoon! Less than forty-five minutes ago, my son was brutally beaten!"

"Your what, ma'am? Your son?"

"Yes, my son. Did you see what went on here?"

"That black kid was your son?"

"Yes, that black kid is my son, my adopted son, and I want to know what you saw."

"Well, lady, I didn't think it was very nice." The young man was no taller than I. He flipped the hair out of his face as he spoke.

"Not very nice! I'll say it was not very nice! My son came home dripping with blood! Do you know the kid who did this to him?"

"Hey, look, lady, I don't want to get involved." He stepped back. I realized I was almost on top of the counter.

"Involved! You're involved whether you like it or not! Do you know the name of that kid?" I could feel my face growing hot and flushed.

"Look, ma'am, he's a rough customer. I don't want to get involved. There could be retaliation."

"Retaliation! Look! I don't know your name, and you don't know mine. All I want is the name of the person who did this to my son! His head was bashed into your Coke machine!"

As I gestured toward the machine, I spied a small TAKE ONE FREE pad attached to its side. It was covered with blood. I tore the first page off and slapped it on the counter under the clerk's nose.

Pounding the paper with my finger, I shouted, "This is my son's blood, and I want to know the kid's name who did this to him!"

In a small voice, he told me.

I felt victorious! I took a pencil from the counter, wrote the name on the blood-soaked paper, and marched out of the store.

On the sidewalk, a neighbor greeted me with a cheerful "Hello."

"Hello," I barked.

I got into the car. The police station, I thought. I must go to the police station before I take Stephen to the hospital.

The two-way radio sputtered as I pushed through the

squeaky wooden screen door. An officer looked up from his desk. I could feel my chin wobble and my eyes begin to fill with tears.

"I'm Mrs. Purdy, the woman who called a few minutes ago about the assault on my son."

"Yes, Mrs. Purdy. We sent an officer over to the shop. Someone mentioned a scuffle, but all seems to be quiet now."

"Quiet?" I slapped the paper down. "This is my son's blood! And this is the name of the man who beat my son. He could have killed him!"

"How do you know the name, ma'am?"

"The clerk told me! He saw the whole thing. I'm so angry I could scream!" I looked for a place to sit.

"Take it easy, ma'am! I know this young man. He's always in trouble."

"I want to press charges. I want him arrested. Racism, that's all it is." Tears ran down my face.

"Sorry, ma'am, we can't arrest him! It's a past crime." The officer shrugged.

"Past crime! You've got to be kidding. Less than forty-five minutes ago, my son was attacked and called a half-pint nigger, and you can't arrest this person?"

"Take it easy, lady. According to the law, unless an officer witnessed this incident, it's your kid's word against that of his attacker."

"But there *is* a witness—the clerk behind the counter!"

"We'll have to subpoena him if you really want to press charges."

"*I want to press charges!*"

"Have you taken your son to the hospital?"

My insides felt like jelly; like waves of nausea, my anger and rage repeatedly ebbed and flowed. I stared at the officer; there was a quickening of understanding between us. I knew what had to be done.

"I'm on my way home now, Officer; the hospital is my next stop. But, sir, I have another black son, and he's out there with a friend looking for that racist bigot! I foolishly asked him to see if he could get the license number of the car. This, of course, was before I knew Stephen had been called a half-pint nigger."

"Don't worry, ma'am. We'll look for them. If you want, you can bring Stephen in to have him photographed for police records."

"I don't want to put him through that, Officer. I've washed away all the blood. I just want a doctor to see him, so it won't be one hysterical mother's word against that kid's!"

The screen door squeaked again as I walked out into blinding sunlight. I realized it was 4:00 in the afternoon. The sky was blue, and it was a beautiful day!

Ronald and his friend were sitting with Stephen when I walked in. A cartoon flickered on the screen.

"Oh, thank goodness you're home! Stephen, come now, we're going to the emergency room." I took one more look at his oozing scalp and helped him to his feet.

"Mom, it hurts to swallow. I can hardly talk." His voice was hoarse, and he was holding his throat.

"Is it because he choked you?"

"Yeah. His arms, Mom—muscles and veins popping out. My feet weren't touching the floor."

David drove up just as we were getting in the car.

"Oh, you're home. Thank goodness! Stephen's had an accident—no, not an accident—he was beaten. Can you drive us to the hospital?"

"An accident! Beaten!" David's expression was incredulous.

"Yes, the whole thing is terrible. Can you drive? I'll tell you all about it on the way."

June 18, 1981

On a bright, sunny afternoon in the middle of a store in downtown Winchester, the unthinkable happened to our family: our 11-year-old son was brutally assaulted and beaten by a young adult twice his size.

My son was looking for a Father's Day card for me when his attacker got out of a car, brazenly walked into the shop, and, lifting the boy off his feet by the throat, nearly choked him to death while beating his head against a soft drink machine.

Several people stood in line at the cash register not five feet away, and no one did anything to stop the attack, or, after his attacker left the store, to assist the injured boy.

This happened not late at night, in a dark alley, at a deserted edge of a playground, but in broad daylight in the middle of one of Boston's "most desirable suburbs" with people looking on who apparently had not even the common human decency to ask the boy if he was all right or needed any assistance.

When my wife called the police, they said that someone had called in about a scuffle and an officer had gone to investigate—restoring to us some faith in human nature.

As citizens of this community, it is equally disturbing to us that as he was being strangled and battered, his assailant said, "You half-pint nigger!" They say history is full of ironies. My son is an adopted Vietnamese orphan, the biological child of a Vietnamese mother and black American father.

When the Vietnam war was winding down six years ago, my son, along with thousands of other children, was put on an airplane and brought to the United States for fear that the orphaned children of American GIs would be poorly treated by the new Communist government. In the USA, it was believed, they would be free, they could live in peace, they would have a chance.

I don't know really how my son would have been treated had he continued to live in his native country—maybe he would have been killed by the Communists, maybe he'd be carrying a gun now as a young military recruit, maybe he'd be doing forced labor in the rice paddies of a government-controlled farm. I tell him that as I try to explain to him why he's better off here.

But that brutal attack on a beautiful June afternoon in one of America's most affluent suburbs causes me to wonder: when citizens stand by and watch without lifting a finger to help, when an 11-year-old is called vicious racist names, is he free, can he be at peace, does he have a chance?

We write this letter in the hope that it will help to remind all of us that none of us lives in peace and freedom when we fail to be responsible to and for one another and when racism continues to bubble beneath the surface waiting for a child to become its target.

Reverend David A. Purdy

THE TRIAL

September 14, 1981

I had just come home from school; I could hear the phone ringing as I opened the door. It was the lieutenant in charge of Stephen's case. They needed Stephen to testify in court the very next day.

When I hung up the phone a heavy sadness came over me. The whole incident must be recalled once more. Months had passed. How much had Stephen forgotten? The details were important. We would need to ask him what he remembered, then remind him of things he had related to us at the time.

September 15

We arrived at the courthouse on time and pushed our way through the crowded hallways. I felt everyone was looking at us. A black couple with a two-year-old sat in one corner of the lobby. Other people stood and talked to attorneys.

Please, Lord, don't let us come face to face with the guy who did this, I thought. Then I saw him, seated near the swinging doors. I shifted my position to shield

Stephen from his view as we walked toward the lieutenant.

"It shouldn't be too long now, Reverend and Mrs. Purdy. Stephen, you will be asked to tell the court exactly what happened the day of June 17. It's important that you recall the details." The lieutenant looked at Stephen kindly. "Take a seat; you never know when they'll call us." He moved away through the crowd.

Black Naugahyde benches with chrome legs bordered the entire lobby. We sat down.

Stephen whispered, "There he is."

"I know, honey." I was beginning to see why people did not want to "get involved." Pressing charges had its price.

"Mom, what if he sees me? What if he grabs me?"

"He won't. He knows he has to be on his best behavior."

David gently rubbed Stephen's shoulder.

The defense attorney approached and introduced himself. "Say, we'd like to settle this whole thing out of court." He ran his fingers through his thick black hair.

"What do you mean by 'out of court'?" David stood up, his eyes fixed on the lawyer.

"We'd like to pay any bills—hospital bills, and so on. How much were they?"

"Our insurance company paid for it," I blurted out.

"How many stitches did he have?" the lawyer pressed on. "The witness from the store seems to think the scuffle wasn't much."

"Wasn't much!" I exclaimed. "He told me himself that the guy was a rough customer, that *he* was afraid of retaliation!" I glanced over and saw the witness sitting amiably with the defendant, but I continued. "You didn't see my son with blood dripping from both elbows as he held his head."

"I'm not saying what he did was right!" He turned to

David. "It says in the Bible that we should forgive and forget, Reverend."

"Forgive and forget? Oh, and what chapter is that from?" David retorted.

Anger ran through me. How dare he pull such an approach!

"Look, the kid's just turned nineteen. What good will it do to give him a criminal record?"

"*I'm* not giving him a criminal record!" David placed his hand on his chest. "*I* didn't beat my son! Look! I play social worker all the time—that's my job—but this time I'm the father of a boy who is the victim of an assault and battery."

"Excuse me," said the lawyer. He held up a finger, asking us to wait a moment. He returned to his client. Stephen looked anxious and confused.

"I can't believe this!" I exclaimed.

The attorney came back. He folded his hands and straightened his shoulders. "We really would like to settle this out of court. How about a donation to the church?"

I jumped to my feet. "You're trying to bribe us!"

David put his hand on my arm to calm me. "We're going to let this case run its course, thank you; any negotiating should have taken place long before this! It's twenty minutes of eleven!"

"Okay, okay." The lawyer gestured with both hands. "Then my client will admit to said facts."

The lieutenant returned. "It's time, ma'am. And by the way, this kid already has a criminal record. This is hardly the first time for him."

The black doors swung open as we all filed in. Overhead, an enormous light flooded the courtroom, so bright it seemed to pulsate through its black framework.

"I will take the stand and present said facts," the lieutenant told us. "Stephen will not need to testify."

The judge, a good-looking older man, sat behind a large bench.

As the lieutenant addressed the judge my eyes wandered. The accused sat with one hand resting on the other; the light from above bounced off his pale blue shirt.

Certain phrases stood out as the lieutenant spoke: " . . . adopted black Vietnamese child . . . eleven years old . . . taken by the throat . . . beat his head . . . Coke machine . . . half-pint nigger!"

The judge leaned forward. "Haven't I seen this kid on probation, Officer?"

"Yes, your honor. His first probation was in 1973."

"Holy smoke—nine years ago! He must have been ten or eleven then. He's no juvenile! Bring me his file."

"Mom, I'm hungry. I don't want to stay here anymore. Can't we go?" Stephen's look was strained.

"Nine probations in nine years. . . . Breaking and entering, starting at ten years of age. Drunken driving . . . driving to endanger. . . . Just off probation!" The judge leaned forward and peered over his glasses.

"There was provocation, your honor—not enough to justify such action—"

Blam, blam! The defense lawyer was cut off.

"Come on, Stephen. Daddy, I'm going to take him for a sandwich; I think he's had enough." We crawled over David's legs and left the courtroom.

We walked on the rainy streets, Stephen six feet ahead of me. Hands in his pockets, he looked down at the pavement.

I loped along. Where were that boy's parents? He had been alone in court!

"There's a McDonald's, Mom. Can we go there?"

"Sure. Go ahead, I'll catch up." Maybe his parents had been through too much. Nine probations in nine years!

When we reentered the courthouse I was relieved to see David standing outside the big swinging doors with the Lieutenant.

"Is it over? Are we through?" I asked.

"Oh boy, is it ever! Three months in the house of correction!"

I was sure David was not as elated as he sounded. Three months in the house of correction? My heart sank.

David continued, "And that's not all. When he was sentenced, his lawyer said, 'Your honor, isn't there any alternative?' and the judge said, 'Yeah, cut off three fingers of his left hand.' He has had it with this kid! He wasn't going to give him an inch."

"Oh, my God," I whispered.

"And that's not all. . . . As the kid left the court-room, he swung his arm way back and smashed his fist into the door right next to me!"

"Ooh, I'm glad I wasn't here," said Stephen.

"The judge yelled at him, 'Come back here! I'm holding you in contempt of court! Stay here for further sentencing.' Well, I'll tell you, I was glad you had taken Stephen out!"

The trial was over.

September 29

The phone rang. It was the District Attorney. He asked if there were some other sentence we would agree to. We were being asked to be judge and jury! Two weeks had passed since the trial. I told him I would talk to David and we would get back to him.

September 29, 1981

Three months in the house of correction were not going to help the boy who had attacked Stephen. David and I had talked earlier of getting in touch with his parents, thinking therapy was the only hope for turning him around.

When we called back, we expressed our desire for mandatory psychiatric help.

Two days later the D.A. returned our call with the final decision. Stephen's attacker was remanded to a full year of weekly therapy. He was to stay away from Stephen, and any violation of this decree—in fact, any violation of the law—would send him directly to jail to serve the original sentence!

NIGHTMARE MINE

February 15, 1982

I sat up and pushed the pillow back under my head. I had just surfaced from the depths of a nightmare. My heart pounded and perspiration ran down my breastbone and into my nightgown. I looked at the clock—3:00 A.M. I felt a sense of relief, knowing the dream was over, but a dimension of undeniable reality remained.

In the dream I had been squatting by a campfire. Other figures were gathered about but darkness made their forms indistinguishable. In my hands I held a large egg. A piece of the shell was broken, exposing the yolk and white. The figure of a woman imposed itself upon me. She kept grabbing the egg and shoving her thumbs into the yolk in an attempt to break it. The yolk, yet unbroken, would roll away from her thumbs. In terror, I would snatch the egg back, shouting, "Please don't hurt it. Please, it isn't cooked yet."

In front of me was a pan of boiling water. Each time I placed the egg in it, slime appeared, and horrid creatures—snakes, lizards, reptiles of all kinds—swam to the surface and attacked the egg. Quickly I would rescue it, throw out the putrid liquid, and replace it with fresh . water. And again the woman would grab the egg.

Who was she? I wondered as I lay back. Her beady eyes had peered through horn-rimmed glasses. Her red hair was drawn back and fastened in the back; kinky, coarse, and long, graying at the temples, it reflected her very personality. Was she the embodiment of all those mothers I had known—all the know-it-all, judgmental, this-is-the-way-to-raise-children kind of mothers? I was sick of them, although I knew I probably had been just like them before Hoāng Stephen's entrance into my life. Because of this child, I would never again be the same.

Was I becoming paranoid? Or did the dominant figure and the reptiles depict racism—its insidious presence, its vicious, unfair attack upon a child who already had so much to deal with? Did my anxiety over the semiraw egg represent my desire for more time? More time for Stephen's adjustment? For my adjustment? For health and wholeness and fairness?

Stephen's nightmares had become mine, his fears and terrors mine. I curled myself around David's sleeping form. How impossible this task would be without him!

WINCHESTER TRACK MEET

<hr />

May 16, 1982

This past fall Stephen had announced that he *must* join the Pop Warner football team. Sports were not a part of David's background, or of mine. We had tried to bridle Stephen's energy with guitar lessons, jazz classes, tap-dance classes—had never thought of sports! How pleased the coaches were to see our strapping twelve-year-old—5'5" and 120 pounds. It all had just happened—a structure, a focus; something Stephen was crazy about.

The other three children had had some successes. Ronald had been cast as lead in *The Hobbit*. Kristen also had been successfully cast. Both girls were good students and loved ballet. Now it looked as though a focus for Stephen was forming.

A birth certificate was required to accompany his football application. Having none, we sent along a copy of his legal birth card. At the very next practice, the coach had come looking for me.

"Mrs. Purdy, we received your son's application and birth card! Tell me something—will this document hold up legally in court? If an official from an opposing team were to question Stephen's age, could we prove it?"

"We've been told that this has the same authority as a

birth certificate. It can be used to obtain a passport, or whatever."

"O.K., that's great! Stephen's quite a boy. He's as big as some of my fifteen-year-olds. As a matter of fact, we probably will have to put him on the A team; Pop Warner has pretty strict rules when it comes to size and weight."

On the way home I had wondered—a legal document. But was he really twelve? Everyone had always wondered about his age. I shared my concern with our doctor on the next visit. Was there any way of really telling? Were all the mysteries surrounding this child frozen in time?

"We could always do a bone chronology scan," the doctor had suggested. "It's simple—an X-ray that shows age by the growth plates in the hand."

The finding: Stephen's X-ray coincided with the listed date of birth, give or take six months. I chuckled that his genetic father could have been as big as Jim Brown or Rosie Grier!

Now it was spring, and on this beautiful, balmy day I was waiting to watch Stephen compete in a 6.2-mile race. The runners were gathering. The officials filled out the proper forms and pinned 42 on the back of Stephen's shirt. His voice interrupted my rambling thoughts.

"Mom, I'll see you at the finish line." He grinned as he continued to stretch first one leg, then the other. "Naturally I'll be there first!"

"Did you weigh yourself today?" I shouted.

"Yeah, 128 pounds."

Bang! The gun went off. I was standing so close the vibration went through me. My throat tightened and tears welled up in my eyes. What a sentimental slob I am, I thought. The theme song from *Chariots of Fire* flowed through my mind. As a family, we had just seen the movie, and Stephen had been inspired. I sputtered an uncontrolled sob. What if he doesn't win? I thought. What if life is too much for him?

David was performing a wedding and I was the only one free to watch the race. I felt lost in the crowd. A sea of life, with Stephen out there somewhere—running, running toward a finish line. How great a distance had this soul come! Not only in miles, but from a culture too ancient for me to comprehend. Lost and separated from his biological mother, he had entered my life. Could I possibly love a child so much? The very pain and suffering he had put me through had been an incredible bonding force. With each centimeter of growth, I had learned to thrill to his accomplishments.

The growing had not stopped, and I was sure the backsliding had not stopped either. But one thing I knew. My love for him was unconditional. No matter what course his life took, I would always love him.

"Hi, Mrs. Purdy." It was a friend of Ron's. "Did Ron go to play practice?"

"Yes . . . yes, he did." I was embarrassed by my tears and quickly looked away.

Stephen came in third in the eighteen-and-under category.

On the way home he said, "Remember the movie, Mom? Every time I rounded a corner, I said, 'God give me the power!'"

How I prayed He would continue to do so!

At home, I found a chain for his newly acquired bronze medal.

"Now," said Stephen. He turned over a wastebasket and stood on it. "Let's pretend this is the Olympics and I'm receiving this for the U.S. of A." He stood there in his running shorts, grinning from ear to ear.

"Wait! I forgot something!" He ran into his room and

started the tape "Chariots of Fire." He jumped back up on the up-ended wastebasket.

"O.K. I'm ready." He bowed to the imaginary crowd.

"And now, representing the United States of America," I announced, "the outstanding winner, Hoāng Stephen Purdy!"

THE SINS OF THE FATHER

November 27, 1982

I restlessly shuffled through page after page of *Good Housekeeping*. A voice broke the silence.

"Mrs. Purdy," said the doctor, "if you'd like to wait with him, he has to lie still for about twenty minutes."

I entered the sterile room, its white walls glistening under the fluorescent light. The weight of Stephen's form crinkled the long strip of white paper. He looked particularly brown as he lay face down. I was not prepared for what I saw. There must have been twenty-five razor-thin stripes, or cuts, in two neat rows up and down his back. He looked as though he had been flogged. At the end of each cut was a drop of fluid.

The doctor moved the crane-necked lamp a little closer to Stephen's back.

"These pin pricks at the end of each marked line; do you see the droplets?"

"Are those cuts in his back?"

"No, no, just pen lines so I can locate each pin prick. Each drop contains allergens to a different food group. There are more than one hundred possible foods he could be allergic to. I have my doubts, Mrs. Purdy, that he's allergic to any of them."

"I know, I know. You said that on the phone. It's just that I've read so much about allergies and child behavior lately. I simply can't leave a stone unturned."

"As an allergist, I think I should tell you that these claims of cures in behavior by simply eliminating a certain food . . . well, the scientific data is very thin."

My thoughts wandered . . . "The sins of the father are visited upon the heads of their children . . . " I never had understood that passage from Scripture; I always deemed it unfair. Now there seemed to be evidence. It was as though there was a hold from Stephen's past—a grip that would not let go, that held him fast, that even my unconditional love could not break.

"Here, use my magnifying glass. There seems to be no swelling, no redness or bubbling." The doctor went on, "If he were allergic to any of these droplets, his blood and body fluids would react. We'd probably see it by now."

"But the mood-swings, Doctor. There are days I just can't stand the anger, the verbal lashing out."

I knew Stephen could hear me loud and clear, but I didn't care. Usually I was very careful to keep these negative thoughts to myself; David and I had always been careful not to "write a script" for Stephen. We had seen so many parents who had drilled into their children's heads that they were "bad" or "impossible." As if programmed, these children, like tape recorders, would play back the expected behavior. Stephen was deeply entrenched in a negative mood-swing at the moment, and he had pulled me down with him. It was all I could do to tolerate his behavior.

"Nothing pleases him; he abuses his brother's and sisters' things, helps himself to whatever he wants in the kitchen. He eats, hungry or not. I bought a bottle of pain tablets the other day. It hadn't been on the kitchen table twenty minutes! He opened it and took two! No thought to what it was!"

"I certainly can sympathize, Mrs. Purdy. These mood-swings? When are his best times?"

"Right now he's between sports; he's through with football and track has yet to begin."

"Can I get up now?" grumbled Stephen.

"Just a minute, son. One last look."

Then the doctor washed Stephen's muscular back with a sterile solution and helped him up. "You can get dressed now."

I walked back to the waiting room with the doctor. Hoping for a "pill" to cure all ills, now I was convinced there was none.

"I'm still looking for answers, Doctor. My husband and I took Stephen to the School Function Clinic at Boston's Children's Hospital about three weeks ago. He had a thorough going-over. No dyslexia of any kind! Above-average I.Q., excellent motor ability, left-footed, right-handed, perfect hearing! But as usual, no answers as to why he is an underachiever!"

"I'm sorry, Mrs. Purdy. Did they give you any diagnosis?"

"Well, finally, Doctor, we demanded an answer! We said, 'Look, you tell us our son is *not* dyslectic, that nothing is wrong with him. He has an above-average I.Q. but is doing poorly in school. Something is wrong; can't you put some label on the problem?' The doctor finally said that if he had to, he would say Stephen has a 'hyperactive attention disorder.'"

"That's general enough."

"Sport seems to be the only vehicle that superimposes a positive self-image. His insides are still so fragile that during just these few weeks . . . I just don't know." Despair was beginning to affect my voice. I felt as if someone were standing on my chest.

"You certainly have your hands full, Mrs. Purdy." The doctor put a comforting hand on my shoulder. Stephen entered the room.

"Mom, can I go ahead and walk home?" The doctor's office was only a few blocks from our house.

"Yes, go ahead. I'll be along in a minute."

"Look at it this way, Mrs. Purdy. No one has found anything wrong with Stephen. If he winds up in a sports career, he may find the disciplined structure, the happiness, the life-style he needs."

"Thank you, Doctor. Thanks for listening!"

I moved on to the receptionist's desk, feeling little better than when I had arrived. I paid the expected fee for the test. How desperate I must be! I thought as I signed the check. I pushed through the swinging doors and walked to my car. I was exhausted.

The stark image of Stephen's back loomed in my mind. It seemed so pathetic. "With his stripes we are healed" (Isa. 53:5 KJV). Could this line of Scripture now floating about in my mind have relevance here? Would there ever be a healing?

I must have switched on the radio without thinking. I was sitting at a stoplight, staring at a woman in the car facing me. She was a mirror image of myself. One human being staring at another, in a seemingly endless line of cars. I shook my head and sighed. Will there ever be an answer, Lord? I felt incredibly lonely.

Then a strange thing happened! The woman I was staring at began to mouth the very song I was listening to. The song was innocuous, of no consequence, but suddenly a chasm of feeling was bridged; her mouth was moving, and the words were coming out of my radio—a connection, a jumping through space! There seemed to be a presence, a strange presence, communicating that my very life and all I was going through somehow counted! The woman sang on, in perfect rhythm with my radio; it was as though my woes, my struggles, were being simultaneously registered in another dimension; beat by beat, pain by pain, I was not alone.

DAY BY DAY

June 16, 1983

I sat wearily in a front pew, camera in hand. I knew this dress rehearsal would be the only time to get pictures. Our youth group was putting on *Godspell*, and all four Purdy children were in it. Ronald had been cast as Jesus and was doing a fabulous job. His full voice was perfect for the part. Having worked on the choreography for many plays, I had been smart enough to step aside on this one! Our ministerial assistant was doing a fine, but uphill job as director, and a super lay member was handling the choreography.

What was it the director had said last week? "This is the first play I've worked with that somehow, there has been no chemistry, no pulling together in a cohesive group!" Stephen's negative attitude was a big part of the problem; Ronald, Jess, and Kristen had complained about it daily. However, several others also had contributed to the splintered feeling!

Lights were being tested all around me. Jessica had a terrible sore throat and was looking for her lozenges. I wondered why I had insisted that all four participate. It was a continual job, trying to persuade Stephen to relate to the rest of the family in any meaningful way.

"O.K., kids, let's begin," the director called out. "Jessica, do the best you can on your solo. Save your voice for opening night!"

The play began with "Prepare Ye," and I was swept away with the music. My biggest sin must be pride, because every time one of my four said a line or sang a solo, a glow came over me.

Kristen came playfully down the aisle in a red hat and blue feather boa, singing "Turn Back, O Man." Jessica managed her "Day by Day" solo. Her face was so beautiful, so sensitive.

How ironic to see Ronald with his striped suspenders and a Superman S on his chest. That very first Halloween, two days after his arrival, we had dressed him as Superman! Now a black Jesus . . . it was so symbolic!

Stephen appeared. "Father, give me my share of the property . . . ."

I had known he was cast as the prodigal son. But now I thought, how fitting.

The narrator read on: "So he divided up his estate between the two of them. Before very long, the younger son collected his belongings and went off to a distant land . . . ."

Stephen, pantomiming the whole thing—something at which he certainly had enough early practice!— jumped up and straddled the board that bridged two saw horses. His acting was fantastic as he stuffed his face and swung his legs in ecstasy. His leopard-print pajama bottoms and General Hospital shirt were comical!

Why had he said earlier that evening, "This play is dumb! It's the last play I'll ever be in!"? He was wonderful!

He went on, "My father's hired men have more food than they can eat, and here am I, dying of hunger!"

Left to Right: Kristen, Ron, Jessica, Hoàng Stephen, David, Pamela (1983)

Narrator: "So he got up and went to his father. . . . "

The older brother spoke: "When this son of yours arrives . . . for him you kill the fatted calf! . . ."

The entire time the older son was speaking, behind his back, Stephen was playing to the audience. Sticking out his tongue and pouting at the brother, winking at the audience, stroking his fine imaginary robe, he was stealing the show. If having "lived a little" enhances one's acting ability, maybe that's what had happened to Stephen.

Ronald rose to sing in full voice, microphone in hand, "When wilt thou save the people, oh God of mercy, when . . . "

I could feel myself being overcome. Tears blurred my vision. Such beautiful kids—I had such beautiful kids! This was an experience I would cherish for years to come. I was totally absorbed for the next half hour! I kept forgetting to take pictures.

Ronald spoke: "I tell you this: One of you is going to betray me. . . . Go quickly and do what you have to do."

The cast sat in a circle at Ronald's feet, sharing and acting out Communion.

"I shall drink no more wine until the kingdom of God comes."

One by one, with "On the Willows" as background music, the members of the cast stood up to say their good-byes to "Jesus." It was so beautiful to see the deep-felt hugging. Jessica rose, pantomiming . . . how moving to see brother and sister hug this way. Kristen did a feather-boa shimmy and hugged Ronald. The tears were really flowing now. Stephen stood up, mimed a hand jive, slapped a five, and hugged his brother.

I couldn't believe what I was seeing! I detected a sob and heave in Stephen's shoulders; he drew apart, sat down. Genuine tears were running down his face! I looked at all the faces; others were in tears as well. But Stephen—I couldn't believe Stephen! Why did he swing from one extreme to the other? I would never know the answer, but thank God Stephen did.

The play ended with Ronald tied to a wire fence and "crucified." The cast climbed ladders and, writhing on them, undulated in agony until finally, strobe lights flashing, full-volume electric guitars wailing, "Christ" was untied, held high, and carried down the aisle. There was not a dry eye in the church. And this was just dress rehearsal!

I was trying to busy myself, collecting props and generally cleaning up, when Ronald and Jess came up to me. Ron spoke.

"Mom, did you believe Stephen—the kid was really crying! I mean he was really sobbing!"

"No kidding!" Jessica emphasized.

"I saw, honey. My own tears were blurring my vision, but I saw. You kids were fabulous; I can't tell you what it means to me to have you four in this play!"

Kristen and Stephen came up, and I hugged them all.

Day by day, I thought, so shall my strength be.

174

MUSWELL HILL, ENGLAND

July 10, 1983

I sat down in the dining room and opened my box of stationery. Sun flooded the table as it poured through leaded-glass Tudor windows. We were here in London, all six of us! We had arranged to swap homes and cars with another pastor and family. It was an inexpensive way to travel and probably, we had surmised, one of the last family trips we would take. Kristen, having just finished her junior year, would work next summer. All four would be in high school in the fall. We had really struggled with the wisdom of bringing Stephen. Six of us, traveling around England in a small foreign station wagon, was not the most exciting thought. A sport camp for the six weeks would cost about the same. Weighing all options, we had chosen to stay a family unit, and here we were.

The light airmail stationery crinkled as I began my letter:

Dear Mom,

Cream teas and scones with jam and whipped cream have become our downfall! Somehow English teacups and Stephen don't mix, and we are delighted when we can find a tearoom with an outdoor serving area. Cathedrals impress Stephen inasmuch as how many football fields can be put into one! Last night in a restaurant (Stratford on Avon) we allowed each of the children to have a little wine. Stephen was a riot! He mimicked the Orson Welles wine commercial— "Ahhhhh (glass swirling under his nose) love that preventation!" Then, taking a sip, he exclaimed, "The condensation is excellent also!" What a character!

Saw Henry VIII *after dinner; Kristen is in heaven with her love of English history. Stephen deliberately sat next to her, "So I can ask her what's going on!"*

The four children went to the Methodist Youth forum this morning. David and I went to church. After the service Jessica laughed, telling me the English kids could not believe they were brothers and sisters. She said they kept saying, "Get away!"

After the church coffee hour, I was introduced to a black woman and her three-year-old son. It's so funny to hear black people speak with an English accent. She was curious about Ronald and Stephen. She is from Ghana and one of sixteen children. My face must have registered pain for her poor mother! She laughed. Her father had two wives, and between the two there were fifteen brothers and sisters. I asked if she could tolerate sharing her husband with another wife, and she said, "No, no! Why do you think I'm living in England?!"

Stephen brought a black kid home the other evening. He had said he was just walking downtown to buy a souvenir at a local store. We were worried when he didn't return for over an hour. Later he told us, with great compassion, that the kid was very poor. He had been to his "flat"; there was no refrigerator and the hallway was full of garbage. He said he almost got sick while watching the kid drink a bottle of curdled milk! The boy had invited

Stephen to spend the following summer with him! He obviously said, "Uh . . . no thanks." David and I fantasized about the trouble he could have gotten into and shared our fears with all the children. Stephen's response was, "What are you worried about? The kid is black!" It makes us wonder if we haven't done too good a job on the race issue!

I finished my letter and reflected. It was amazing that Stephen was still so at home in the streets.

July 17

Dear Mom,

So great of you to call on David's birthday last night! It was so good to hear your voice. So unbearably hot here (90s), we can't believe it. This summer is breaking all kinds of records when it comes to heat! As I told you on the phone, our trip to a cooler climate took us to a coastal town called Weston-Super-Mare. It was not Cape Cod! Coney Island all the way, casinos, video games, and huge muddy beaches. We got right back in the car, in spite of a great protest from Stephen. Continuing southwest, we finally came to a town called Minehead, an improvement, but not much better. We checked into a bed-and-bath run by a good-looking Italian woman. She really was the Sophia Loren type! Stephen, right away, pressed her on her cooking abilities. She looked at David and me and said, "Sure is a cheeky devil!"

Later, getting on bathing suits ("babing pant," according to Stephen), Jessica got locked in the bathroom. I don't know what the poor woman must have been thinking. She was so panicked—ran outside with a key, planning on throwing it up to the window, but alas, Jessica couldn't open it. Finally, Jess managed to work the latch into an open position.

The beaches of Minehead were so filthy and muddy

177

(they need a bottle bill here). The tide goes so far out that the next morning we decided to continue even farther down the coast. We were so glad we did; we came upon a little town called Lynton. The area is called the English Switzerland. High above this town is another called Lynmouth. Flowers, sheep, mountains, and valleys. Unfortunately, the beaches were not much better; then we made a discovery. Running from the mountains through the village, and on out to sea, was a fresh-water trout stream, only it wasn't just a stream! Walking far enough inland along cobblestoned banks and walkways, it became rapids! It was so hot that in minutes the kids were wading, and in no time we were all swimming in the freshest, cleanest water I'd ever seen! Jessica went in dressed in shorts! We could lie on our backs and ride the current over smooth rocks.

The English people are wonderful! They are so reserved. We soon realized that we had an audience from a roadway high above the river. First two elderly ladies made their way down to the water's edge; then a few more. There was some tittering, and next thing we knew, shoes were being removed and some of the ladies were wading.

Later that morning as we made our way through the town to go to lunch, an Englishwoman stopped me. "Can you tell me where the Americans are swimming?" she asked.

I chuckled to myself as I gave her directions to the rapids. As they walked away, one of them remarked about how "spontaneous" Americans are.

July 22

Dear Mom,

Just mailed you two postcards this morning, saying they would probably be the last communications from me

until we touch down at Logan. Here I am writing again!
I'm lying in the sun in this tiny backyard surrounded by
roses! I must share with you some of the events of the past
few days in Paris! Please save these letters for me.

We crossed the English Channel in gorgeous weather!
It was so unusually beautiful that almost everyone went
topside mid-trip. One could see the White Cliffs of Dover
on one side, Calais on the other. When we arrived at our
hotel in Paris (one star) Stephen immediately used the
bidet as a urinal. He said, "What the . . . !" as it
splashed all over him.

Riding the underground in France is quite the
experience. Jessica and Kristen were helping Stephen
with simple French sentences because he was dying to
talk to some "ooh la las." We were hysterical coming
home late one night as Stephen told a girl it had been very
hot—"Je . . . suis chaud" [I am hot].

Later, between stops, a falling-down drunk saw me
talking to Ronald; we were all standing, hanging on to
overhead railings. I don't know what he must have been
thinking, but as he slurred and drooled in French,
shouting louder and louder, Stephen made his way over
to us, David close behind.

"Mom, is this guy bothering you?" He glanced at the
man.

"Just ignore him, Stephen. He's drunk."

"I'll deck him if he lays a hand on you!"

Ron spoke up. "Stephen, he's too drunk to know what
he's doing."

Just then the train stopped, the door opened, and we
were out! I was touched by Stephen coming to my defense
like that.

In four days we really did cover ground. Took a boat
tour on the Seine, went to the Louvre, and walked,
walked, walked!

We really must be a curiosity, being a racially mixed

family. More than once people have asked if they can take pictures of us. People hear the boys call us Mom and Dad and are instantly curious.

Two gorgeous black women sat with us on the train on our way back from Paris. The four seats on either side of the aisle face one another. Because there were six of us, David, Ron, Jess, and Kristen sat on one side, Stephen and I on the other. That left two seats for these women to sit with us.

One of the women spoke English and would interpret to the other what Stephen was saying. He asked if the French one was a Paris model; she had numerous tiny braids all over her head and was very beautiful. She laughed shyly said, "No." Before they got off the train they asked if they could take pictures of our family.

One other funny incident, and then I must close. Still on the train, David had just admonished Stephen for the 99th time about not talking so loudly (people were sleeping).

David was commenting on how reserved and quiet the English are, when all of a sudden a woman came racing down the aisle after her husband, screaming, "Wait!"

Next thing we heard was, "Damn, you're bloody deaf!"

Well, I'll tell you, we were absolutely hysterical; even after another hour had passed, one of us would start to laugh. It was so funny!

Can't believe our six weeks are almost over! See you in the States.

Love,

Pam

HIGH SCHOOL OPEN HOUSE

October 4, 1984

More than a year had gone by since our trip to England. The summer just past had been a hard one, but now all the children were back in school, and David and I were making our way through the crowded hallways of Winchester High School. I looked at my watch—7:30 P.M.

"At least Kristen being in college this year makes it a bit easier," I said.

Open house had been a real hassle last year, as we had tried to follow the schedules of four children. During ten-minute intervals, parents were expected to attend their child's (or children's) classes, condensing a six-hour day into an hour and a half. Stephen and Jessica were now fifteen and sophomores. Ronald, a junior, had just turned sixteen.

We compared the first three periods. By eliminating study halls and gym, we would be able to attend most of the academic classes.

"I'd like to visit Stephen's basic English," I said. "Ron has a gym class, so you could go to Jessica's French!" David agreed, and we ran farther down the list, marking the classes each of us would attend.

The bell rang. "Hang on, here we go!" David began looking for room numbers. "I'll see you later."

I worked my way through hallways and up stairways. I felt victorious when I found room 30.

"Come in and sit down, folks. Your son or daughter has me this semester for English. Even though this is a basic-skills class, the students are using the computer. On this desk you will find a disk that stores your child's most recent essay. Just feed the disk into the disk drive—like so—push this button, and you will see the essay on the screen. By the way, the assignment was to write a descriptive paper on how they spent the summer."

Sarcastically I thought, You mean this *last* summer?

H. S. Purdy

IT'S SUNNY OUT AND THE BIRDS ARE SINGING ON THE LIMBS OF THE TREES. I WAKE UP TO THE SUN'S RAY GLISTENING IN YOUR EYE'S. I ROLL OUT OF BED TO SMELL THE SWEET SMELLS OF THE SALTY BEACH. I WALK DOWN STAIRS TO THE KITCHEN TO GET SOME FOOD IN MY EMPTY STOMACH. AS I SIT AT THE TABLE, I SEE POP UP ON THE LATER PAINTING THE WINDOW PAINE, IN HIS OLD FADED SHORTS. PEOPLE WALK BY IN ENVY OF THE NINETEATH CEMTRY COLONEAL HOME ON THE WATER FROUNT. GORDEN AND GREIG ARE HONKING OUT FROUNT IN THEIR "68" CAMAREO FOR ME TO HURRY ME UP TO GO TO THE BEACH. I PUT THE LAST PICE OF TOAST INTO MY MOUTH, GRAB MY "PANAMA JACK" SUN TAN LOTION AND TOWEL, SLAM SHUT THE SCREEN DOOR, AND HOOP IN THE "68", THEN PEAL OUT, LEAVING A FEW INCHES OF RUBBER ON THE DRIVE WAY.

IT'S ABOUT 5:30 P.M. AND I'M JUST ABOUT GETTING HOME FROM THE BEACH AND I CAN SMELL MOM'S FRANKS COOKING OUT BACK ON THE GRILL. I HOP INTO THE OUT DOOR SHOWER TO RINSE OFF SAND AND SALT ON MY BACK. I GO INTO MY ROOM AFTER I SHOWER TO GET SOME DRY CLOTHES ON, AND HERE THE SOUNDS OF THE BEACH BOYS ON THE RADIO.

THE END

I couldn't believe what I was reading. Stephen's memory and my memory of the same summer couldn't have been more different! I read again and reread. Besides the fact that the essay exhibited the usual horrendous spelling, I was struck by its sensitivity. Images of "Pop on a later (sic), in his old faded shorts" and myself in the backyard "cooking franks" were so sweet. Stephen's keen senses of touch, taste, and smell had helped him write this essay.

I felt myself literally shaking my head as images from my own memories surfaced. At the Cape, Stephen had gotten to know several older boys with cars, and we had spent the entire summer worrying, chastising, arguing. There were late nights and heated arguments.

One afternoon I had come home from an art show to find that Kristen had driven Stephen to the local fire station for first aid. Seems he had met a girl riding by on a moped, had borrowed it, ridden around the house, and crashed into the side of the porch. The moped's rear-view mirror had broken and glass was scattered everywhere.

"Mom, the man at the fire station thinks Stephen needs stitches! He thinks we ought to take him to the emergency room."

I sat down on one end of the couch, exhausted. I had just completed twenty-three charcoal sketches at the art show! There lay Stephen, with a blood-soaked bandage. We exchanged some angry words. Then with a sigh, I said, "O.K., Stephen. We'd better get that stitched up."

"It's all right, Mom. I don't need stitches."

"Oh yes you do!" *And I hope it hurts*, I thought in anger.

Kristen offered to drive, and I watched her as we rode in silence. Such a mature, responsible person she'd grown into! How I loved her for it!

Later that day we learned that Stephen's older friends had brought liquor to the house. I was so hurt and angry, I had tried to call the parents of one boy to let them know of the incident; I even drove to their cottage, but as luck would have it, the family had left for home that evening. Stephen had been in no condition to ride that moped; thank God he had ridden it only around the yard! It was no wonder the doctor had questioned his reflexes; she kept looking into his eyes, saying, "Stephen, are you sure you didn't hit your head?"

On another summer evening, Stephen had arrived home in a friend's car at 6:00 P.M. after surfing at the beach most of the day. He was supposed to be at work with his brother, washing dishes in a local restaurant.

He went running into the house. "I have to call work and tell them I'm not coming in."

From the front yard, I called after him, "Stephen, you *are* going to work, and you're already late. They're counting on you."

His hand on the phone, he continued to yell. *"Mom, I don't have to work if I don't want to!"*

With that I went up to the friend who had driven him home. "I'm sorry, but since Stephen's been gone most of the day—"

Stephen was instantly back out in the driveway. His verbal blasts felt as if they came from a human machine gun.

"Mom, we met these kids in Orleans—"

I shot back, *"Stephen, you are not going out, and that's final! If you don't go to work, you're not going anywhere!"*

David had been on a ladder in the backyard. He heard the commotion and rounded the corner just as Stephen kicked an empty plastic trash barrel across the driveway. Then he kicked his friend's car.

"O.K., Stephen, that's enough! Go to your room and cool off!"

David's vacation was almost over, and I dreaded being a single parent for three weeks in August.

After talking it over, David and I had decided: No more cars! And Stephen was grounded for the remainder of the summer. Wherever David went, Stephen would go also. When David went home in August, Stephen was to go with him. If David came down to the Cape for a day or two, he'd bring Stephen. We had a long, very tearful talk and expressed our deep disappointment.

"I don't think you realize," I said, "how violated I feel, Stephen. Daddy and I provided you with a beautiful summer home, and what did you do? A few weeks ago you allowed those boys to sit on *our* porch and drink, and you *joined* them!" Stephen wiped away tears.

"Stephen, we have had many conversations about drinking and drugs. It takes guts to say no, and you've acted like a wimp, allowing those guys to manipulate you! You're an athlete; you've always agreed that you must take care of your body!"

Sobbing, Stephen broke in. "I know you guys won't believe me, but I didn't mean to disappoint you. I love you and . . . " He was crying too heavily to continue.

I got up, tears flowing down my face, and embraced him. I looked into his face.

"Stephen, Daddy and I will always love you, no matter what—but it hurts, it really hurts.

"We believe in you, Stephen. Sometimes I wonder why, but then I remind myself of all your good qualities—the weekends when you took your lunch to Walter and bought him a pint of milk. I didn't know Walter was in his eighties and you were worried that he did not eat regularly." Stephen had learned that Meals on Wheels did not deliver on Saturdays and Sundays.

"Then there was that Vietnam vet on the beach. He

poured out his troubles to you for two hours, and you didn't have the heart to turn your back on him."

After that conversation, Stephen's behavior improved considerably. He certainly wasn't the first teenager to try alcohol. And he actually enjoyed going back and forth to Winchester. August football practice had started, and that helped! He and his Pop had many a good conversation and bachelor trip to the supermarket.

I read the essay one more time. I loved it; it was a real treasure.

"Excuse me. Is there any way to get a copy of this?"

"Sure, Mrs. Purdy, we can get a printout. Stephen is a sensitive writer, if we can just get him focused!"

I sighed. "How well I know!"

"Mrs. Purdy, I'm encouraging parents to write a message on the bottom of these essays. The students will read them tomorrow."

"Oh, I'd like that!" Now let's see, I thought—then I typed in: Stephen, love this essay. Your English teacher is right—you are a good writer! I love you. Mom.

VALLEY FORGE MILITARY ACADEMY

February 3, 1985

The trip to Wayne took more than six hours; we were about halfway there when we stopped at a toll booth on the Pennsylvania Turnpike.

The car had become a think tank for me over the years—at times, a torture chamber. With David usually doing the driving, I would rock along, with time to think, pray, and sort things out. Sometimes I would imagine transcending this metal capsule. I would soar way above it, following the tiny car. My problems did not look so big from up there; many moving cars were to be seen from that height, all swarming along the highway like so many ants going about their business. Then I would mentally come back and begin again to grapple with a problem.

The Marines, I thought. Why would Stephen want so desperately to become a Marine? The question had rolled around in my mind repeatedly for more than a year now. Stephen had come home one night from a friend's house, having seen *First Blood*. Sylvester Stallone, as a Green Beret, singlehandedly had held off an army! Stephen was impressed when Stallone was forced to hunt for his food and then sewed up a gaping wound in his own arm!

187

"Green Bereting it" had become a common expression at our house. Stephen started the phrase himself while drinking plain white milk one day. Having always hated milk, he grimaced and gulped it down.

"I'm Green Bereting it! The coach says I need to drink milk!"

After that it became *our* expression. There were extremes: If Stephen didn't want to go to the dentist or clean up something he had spilled, we'd say "Green Beret it, Steve!"

It was an interesting dichotomy. On the one hand he lifted weights, swaggered around, and acted macho; on the other, at times he was fastidious. He might use five to seven napkins at one meal, not wanting to reuse one. He was forever pulling a clean towel out of the drawer in the kitchen. He took only showers now, afraid of someone else's germs in the tub. If he thought Ronald had breathed on his food, he'd blow the germs off before he ate and guard the rest of his meal with his arms. Sometimes it became ridiculous! Stephen would retaliate by blowing on Ronald's food; then the two boys, arms locked about their plates, would blow rapid fire at each other.

I guess it's called compensation. I wondered how many men had joined the armed forces because of a need to cover up fears, compensate for insecure feelings. What better way to put on protective armor than to don a uniform and become part of a powerful army?

The idea of a military academy had come about as a kind of compromise. Report after report had come from school, stressing the need for structure; a more disciplined private school seemed to be the answer; and the military highly appealed to Stephen.

Now I had to wrestle with my own feelings. Would the military crush Stephen's personality into a "yes sir, no sir" obedient robot type? We would see; this trip could be the answer. If Stephen stayed at the local high school he would talk of nothing but "joining up" at graduation. I cringed at the thought of his life going full circle, being snatched from one war-torn country only to die in another.

David and I had come full circle as well—from our antiwar-protest days to considering a military school for one of our children!

It was 6:00 P.M. when David, Stephen, and I wearily checked into the hotel.

"Yes, my name is Purdy. I have reservations for three," said David.

The woman at the desk handed him a key. "Third floor, Mr. Purdy."

"Dad, give me the key. Let me go up ahead of you guys. I'll pretend I'm here for a track meet!"

At fifteen, he still loved to fantasize! David handed him the key. Stephen picked up his gym bag and swaggered over to the elevator.

David chuckled and shook his head as he paid for the room. After waiting a deliberate few moments, we boarded the elevator. We walked down the corridor and found the right room.

"David," I whispered, putting my back to the wall on one side of the door. I knocked and held my hands in the shape of a gun. David dropped the luggage and did the same. We tried not to laugh; Stephen had done this countless times, playing Magnum, P.I.

Stephen opened the door. "Freeze!" we both shouted, pointing our imaginary guns.

"Oh! Don't do that!" He grabbed at his chest and stumbled backward. Then, quickly regaining his composure, "How do you like my suite?"

"Hey, pretty nice, guy," said David. The TV was already going. "All the comforts of home!"

David and I stretched out on one of the beds; it had been a long trip. The interview was scheduled for 9:00 A.M. the following day.

Stephen picked up the phone and dialed, putting his feet up on a table.

"You're not really dialing," I said.

"Hello?"

"You're not calling Winchester, are you?" I assumed it was still gametime.

"Oh, he's not home? O.K., tell him I called."

I recognized the voice of a woman in Winchester!

"What did you do? Call long distance?" I was really angry.

"What do you think you're doing!" yelled David.

Stephen looked puzzled. "It's not a pay phone. Look, it tells you how to dial long distance."

"What do you mean? We have to pay for that call! They'll bill it to our room."

"Oh, I didn't know," said Stephen in a somber voice.

"Somehow you're going to have to get your compulsive behavior under control!"continued David. "I don't believe you did that!"

I lay back down. Compulsive behavior? That was one reason we were here!

February 4

We entered the administration building and were shown directly to the admissions office.

The major shook our hands warmly and patted Stephen's shoulder, taking note of his size.

Tim Conway, I thought to myself—round face and kind eyes, the guy looks like comedian Tim Conway! His closely cut hair, uniform, and polished shoes were all in order.

The admissions office was beautiful. Celery-green

carpet ran wall to wall beneath our feet. Pictures of cadets in military dress, football teams, autographed photos lined the walls.

"So you folks are interested in Valley Forge."

"Yes," replied David, "for a variety of reasons."

"Stephen, is this your decision to possibly come to Valley Forge?"

"Yes. I want to join the Marines someday, and I think this would be good training."

"Why do you want to be a Marine?"

"They're tough . . . I don't know!" shrugged Stephen. "Why are *you* asking me that?!"

"I've been a Marine! I see by your application you were born in Vietnam. I served in Vietnam. I also attended this school." The major swung around in his chair and pointed out the window. "You see that fence way down at the end of the field? After one week here, I found myself jumping that fence and running away. But where was I to go?" He swung back in his chair. "You think the Marines are tough! This place is tougher!"

Stephen's face was pensive as he cupped his chin in his palm.

"Major," I broke in, "it's academics that *we* are most concerned about. Stephen needs a structure within which he can achieve!"

"I see by your jacket, Steve, you're into football! You must be good, to have earned a varsity letter as a sophomore! What position do you play?"

"Running back and linebacker."

"He's a good player," added David. "He's good at track as well. He always dreamed of playing in the N.F.L.—until recently, anyway."

"Let's see where you stand on our entrance exam, Stephen."

"Exam? Now?" said Stephen.

"Sure, it will take only about a half hour. Then we'll know what we're talking about!"

"You always do well on these kinds of tests." I spoke to Stephen reassuringly. "It's based on your natural intelligence!"

They left the room and David and I stared at each other. This honesty and straight talk were more than I had hoped for. The major rejoined us.

I began, "I'm afraid Stephen has been influenced by these TV ads! You know—the ones where Marines are jumping out of helicopters before breakfast? Then they ride off into the sunset that evening on a motorcycle with some beautiful girl."

"I know the ads," replied the major. "That's not the Marines—I can tell him."

"I might mention here," said David, "that we have some serious financial concerns." He went on to discuss our financial situation, with one child in college, and now possibly another in a private school next year.

"I can understand your concern, Reverend Purdy. I know teachers and clergy are not the highest paid people in this country. In case you don't know, I am the football coach here. If Stephen does well on his entrance exam, I think we can set aside, say . . . a $2,000 scholarship for next year."

I was elated.

"Let's see if he's finished. I'll check his score, and then we can talk further."

The major left the room and returned in a few moments with Stephen.

"Let's see how you've done." A punched card was superimposed on the test and it was quickly graded. "Your score is 62!"

"Just 62? That's a D!" exclaimed Stephen.

"No, that's not how it works. Out of a possible 100, 50

is an average score. This means that 62 is 12 points above average!"

"All right!" Stephen uttered a big sigh.

"You could do very well here at Valley Forge." The phone rang. "One minute, please, while I take this call. Yes . . . And the University of Connecticut as well? That's wonderful! . . . Tomorrow? Yes, I think I can see you tomorrow—2:00? . . . Fine. Bye now.

"Now there's a happy parent. That woman's son has just been offered his second college football scholarship. I'm meeting with them tomorrow to help them decide which one to accept."

"Oh, wow!" said Stephen.

"Back to your interest in the Marines, Steve. A full 96 percent of our graduating seniors choose not to go into the military!"

"Why?" Stephen looked incredulous.

"Because they've had enough of shining shoes, taking orders, and room inspection. I don't think any of the cadets on this campus would tell you they like it here. Many are classic underachievers like yourself. They know they need structure and discipline to succeed. They stay here because we've shown them by improved grades that they *can* achieve!"

"What do you mean—structure?" inquired Stephen.

"O.K. Now, what do your evenings at home look like? Do you watch TV, talk on the phone, listen to the stereo? When do you do your homework? And how much time do you spend on it?"

Stephen grinned and shrugged his shoulders.

"You see, here at Valley Forge we have a rigorous routine. Your day starts at 6:00 A.M. and ends after dinner with a two-hour supervised study hall. You and your roommate sit at your desks in the evening; a faculty member is in the corridor and stops in on you every fifteen minutes or so. You will be asked 'Cadet

Purdy, do you need any help with your homework this evening?' and you will answer either 'No sir, thank you' or 'Yes sir, I have a question regarding biology.' Now, how much room is there for failure?"

"Two hours every night?" Stephen's forehead displayed a mass of wrinkles as his eyebrows knitted.

"Come on, let's take a tour of the campus." The major put on his military overcoat. "I'll show you around one of the dorms."

I was overjoyed. Here was an environment such as David and I could not possibly supply.

We walked along beautiful brick paths between buildings. Two clean-cut cadets approached us. They saluted as they marched by.

"Good morning, Major. Good morning, ma'am, sir."

David glanced at me. It was impressive to be treated with such respect! We entered one of the brick dorms.

"Good morning, Cadet. Would you mind if I showed your room to some visitors?"

"Yes, sir. That would be fine, sir," saluted the young cadet.

We walked into a small room with one window. There were no curtains; a bunk bed ran almost the entire length of the room. An open closet revealed military dress uniforms, all in display order. Even underwear and socks were neatly folded and stacked on open shelves!

"Stephen, as a new cadet, you will take orders from a company upperclassman—someone who has earned the privilege of such rank. Do you think you can take orders?"

"Sure, why not?"

"I'll give you an example. A scrawny little wimp of a guy with thick glasses comes into your room to do inspection one morning. He looks over your bed, picks at the covers, and says, 'Cadet Purdy, I don't like the way you've made your bed.' Then he pulls the bedding, mattress and all, and dumps it on the floor. He says, 'Make it again.' How are you going to react?"

"I'll kill him!" said Stephen, nostrils flaring.

"Ah, but you can't! The only acceptable response is 'Yes sir, I'll do it again, sir!' If you respond any other way, there are demerits; if you accumulate 25 demerits, then marching time on the field is required. Now, is that tough enough for you?"

Stephen glanced at me, then at David.

"After two weeks of football camp in August, there will be six weeks of boot camp. You may write home at that time, but you may not phone or have any visitors. See this bathroom right across the corridor from this room? During boot camp, if this happened to be your room, you wouldn't be allowed to simply cross the hall and enter. You'd have to 'square corners'—you'd march down one side of the hall, square the corner, and march back up the hall to the bathroom. Everyone on this floor would do the same; no one is privileged because of proximity to this bathroom."

"What if I wait until 2:00 A.M. and no one is looking?" replied Stephen.

"Take your chances, Steve, but if you're caught you'd receive demerits. Accumulate enough demerits and you're off the football team. Academically, the same; this is not a school that allows participation in sports if you are not doing well with your subjects."

"What if I'm the best player on the team and could make the difference between winning and losing?"

"Makes no difference. You wouldn't play, and you can bet the rest of the team would be mad as hell at you for those demerits!"

"Oh my God," said Stephen under his breath.

I could not have been happier. He would have to learn some self-control and self-discipline. But could he do it? I was imagining hours of marching, endless demerits. On the other hand, there were rewards. I had read in the catalog of levels of rank earned by the good cadet—uniforms with stars and stripes I knew Stephen would be so proud to wear.

He turned to me. "Mom, you know all the 'yes sirs' and 'no sirs'? Remind me not to do that when I come home on vacation."

"I will not!" I laughed.

For the next half hour we walked the campus, seeing classrooms, athletic facilities, and a magnificent ballroom complete with crystal chandeliers. Classes in character and social etiquette were described, along with karate, riflery, a mounted cavalry, *and* required Sunday chapel.

We left the campus and began our journey home.

"Do you think you want to attend there, Stephen?" I asked. "You know it has to be your decision finally." I was praying he would say yes.

"I don't know, Mom. I'd like to give it a few weeks and then decide."

"O.K. It's up to you."

We rode along in silence for about ten minutes.

"Mom, Dad, you know this could be the opportunity of a lifetime. How soon after I complete my application do you think I'll hear if I'm accepted?"

"Oh, maybe a couple of weeks, honey."

March 22

Stephen received his letter of acceptance from Valley Forge.

REPORTING TO VALLEY FORGE

The temperature was supposed to reach 97 today and tomorrow. What a day to be leaving beautiful Cape Cod on our way *south* to Pennsylvania. For most cadets, August 24 was the first day of school; but here we were, car packed, headed for Valley Forge football camp.

I had had mixed emotions all summer about sending Stephen off to a boarding school. For all the ups and downs, noise and commotion, I would miss him terribly. I felt I was headed for a classic mid-life crisis. David and I would be losing the four children, four Septembers in a row—Kristen last September, now Stephen to Valley Forge, Ronald off to college next year, and Jessica the next. I couldn't imagine an empty nest so quickly. I found myself staring out the car window as we drove along. How quiet the house would be!

It was 95 when we stopped at a picnic area somewhere in Connecticut. Stephen had been unusually quiet. I pulled my sweaty terrycloth sundress away from my body. We were all soaked. We spread an old bedspread under a shade tree; bugs buzzed in the sweltering air around us.

"I can't believe all this heat, Mom!" Stephen sprawled out on his back.

I shook my head. "I know, honey. It's brutal to have to go through football training in this weather."

We had been told that Stephen would be issued his uniform upon arrival, and all his civilian clothing would be handed back to us when we departed. It all seemed so cold, so institutional. I hoped we were doing the right thing. He had been in an orphanage the first five years of his life; were we returning him to another institution?

Hours passed, and we were on the Cross-Bronx Expressway—such heat, stop-and-go traffic! Miles of asphalt surrounded slums, tenements, dirt, and more heat.

"Mom . . . Dad, how do people stand living here in the summer?" Stephen's voice was pensive as he lay back with his bare foot stuck out an open window.

"They have no choice," David answered. "They're poor, and they have no choice."

How blessed we are to have the Cape all summer! I thought. The oppression seemed to intensify with every mile. Steel girders, underpasses, like giant radiators, captured and reflected enormous waves of heat.

Once in a while I noticed, however, that a green weed or a struggling locust tree had projected itself up and out of the rubble. We drove on through five-lane traffic, metal barricades, filth, discarded tires, broken mattress springs—the most inhospitable environment, and yet there was life!

Such a metaphor for the grace of God's love, I thought—such unconditional love! I began actively looking for anything green, anything growing. Was there comfort for me here, a message that no matter how hard boot camp and plebe training, nothing would separate Stephen from the love of God?

August 15

At 10:00 A.M., after a night of air-conditioned sleep, some good food and laughs, we arrived at Valley Forge. In spite of the heat, David was in tie and shirt, I in dress and heels—"respectful attire," according to school rules.

We drove through the impressive gate and were directed to a parking area by a young cadet. Stephen was so silent I turned to make sure he was still in the car.

"Do you have your keys, Stephen, for your foot-locker and cash box?" I didn't know which of us was more nervous.

"Yes, Mom."

"Did you put them on your new key chain?"

"Mom, I can't let anyone see that. I have to start out slow, humble, then make my way to the top."

"O.K." One of Stephen's going-away gifts was a brass key chain with Damn I'm Good inscribed on it. I guess it didn't fit the image of a plebe.

"Mr. and Mrs. Purdy, Stephen." The major shook hands. "Have you been lifting this summer, Stephen?"

"Yes, sir. I have, sir." I loved the response!

"Here are your papers, and if you'll head over to the cadet store, a gentleman will see to it that you receive your uniform and supplies."

"In all this heat, is any heavy workout planned for today?" I asked.

"No, ma'am, we'll go easy on the boys. After mess at noon, we'll do some simple exercises, and then time them on a one-mile run." Shocked, I wanted to ask more, but Stephen began to pull me along.

"Thank you, Major, it's good to see you again," I said and, with swollen feet, clopped along in my high heels as Stephen took the lead.

Everywhere on the immaculate campus cadets were shining brass doorknobs and fixtures. "Old" cadets, lined up in parade formation, all had the same closely cropped hair; all were dressed in khaki shorts, white Valley Forge T-shirts, black shoes, athletic socks.

We entered the store. Cadets were everywhere. I was delighted to see that their uniform clothing was in direct contrast to the diversity of their accents and racial backgrounds.

A black clerk with wire-rimmed glasses took Stephen's list. He handed us a large, brown-paper-wrapped parcel, then proceeded to take Stephen's measurements. Soon we were back out and into the broiling sun. Cadets marched past us as we returned to the major.

"Stephen, Wheeler Hall will be your dorm during football camp." The major gestured behind him. "Mr. Purdy, if you want to bring your car right up to that door, one of the cadets on duty will show Stephen where to put his things."

Stephen and I entered Wheeler Hall and were directed down the corridor.

"This is it," said the cadet on duty. We stood in the doorway of a clean, simple room—one double-bunk bed, two desks, two chairs. Stephen was instructed to open his parcel and dress in summer uniform. I waited in the hall.

When Stephen emerged he looked like all the other cadets, except for his hair! Outside, we sat on a stone wall and waited for his turn with the barber. David returned just in time to hear the name *Purdy* called. Stephen had been with the other young men, meeting their sisters and girlfriends, but now he came to his feet.

David was still out of breath. "One of the cadets helped me move the footlocker into Wheeler. It must be 95 now!"

"It's hard at first," said a mother sitting next to me. I was not aware that I looked so concerned.

"At least he has ten days of football camp to ease into things," David replied.

The woman continued, "Yes, that is one nice way to enter Valley Forge. You know he won't be allowed to call home during the six weeks of boot camp. He can write to you, but he can't call. Send him some baked goods and lots of mail, and he'll make it."

Again, I was terribly afraid we were reinstitution-alizing Stephen. From an orphanage to this.

"Does your son like it here?" I pressed on.

"Like it? No, I wouldn't say he likes it, but he respects it. The school has done a lot for him. His grades are so much improved."

"Hey, there he is!" pointed David. "Or is it . . . ?"

"Sure it is . . . I think." I strained to get a better look at the young cadet approaching us. Stephen had been a full half hour in the barber's chair.

"Stephen, is it you?" said David.

"I can't get used to it, Dad." Stephen kept rubbing his head.

I couldn't decide whether he looked older or younger. Images of a five-year-old "chaldritz," hair shaved off, standing at Logan Airport, flashed to mind. But a strapping, mature cadet stood before me.

"Mom, it took him forever to cut my hair. He kept cutting and cutting. The floor was two feet deep with hair when he finished!"

We returned to the dorm, and one of the "old" cadets helped us collect Stephen's civilian clothes. I could feel a lump in my throat. I knew that in moments we would be saying good-bye. Stephen's amber eyes were watery as they looked into mine.

"That's it, Reverend and Mrs. Purdy. Stephen can go to second mess now. See you Parents' Weekend?" The major shook our hands.

I was startled by his abruptness. "Can parents have lunch with their sons?" I asked, hoping to delay our departure.

"No, it's really better if parents leave at this point. Stephen will be fine."

We embraced Stephen—David first, then me.

"I love you, Mom, Dad."

Stephen's hug lifted me from the pavement, then he quickly turned and was off. With jogging strides, he joined the other cadets and disappeared from sight.

There I was, my face turning to mush, a blue oxford shirt and a pair of chino pants in my hands. David put his arm around me. Thank God for David! I could only think, for I couldn't speak, God be with you, dear Stephen.

EPILOGUE

The morning after Thanksgiving is a wonderful day for me. Mom, who lives right around the corner from us at the Cape, had done her usual herculean task of cooking and baking. Now, the big feast over, the next few days will be relaxing. The house is full of kids and plenty of "fix your own" leftovers.

I love our kitchen here on Cape Cod, with its small cathedral ceiling. As the coffee perks, my eyes move from corner to corner, taking in the work David and I have done. Over the corner cabinet, a Tiffany-style lamp hangs at eye level. My dad discovered this treasure at a flea market, bought it, and accidentally broke it. I had taken a course in stained glass, so the twenty-six amber and green pieces were carefully cut and replaced.

In another corner, sun slices an angular path across a wall-hung pie cupboard. During one of our moves we found it in the basement, covered with paint and filled with jars of nails, but the original white porcelain knob was still in place. Refinished, it is decked with small brass vases, bayberry, and dried herbs, and at the moment is overloaded with breads, pies, and cakes.

When we bought this house the kitchen was very rough. David and I completely redid the ceiling, walls, and floor. The easy-sweep terra-cotta tiles we installed on floors and counter tops give a warmth to the room; the rustic ceiling beams were salvaged from beneath the old porch when it was rebuilt.

I pour two cups of coffee and walk to our bedroom, a few steps from the kitchen. The room is flooded by sheets of blazing sun, magnified by yellow and red calico wallpaper.

I stand and stare at the sleeping form before me. I hesitate to wake David. I place his cup on the night table and sit on the white wicker chair near the bed. I am flooded with happiness. To have all my children under one roof again is wonderful.

The room still has the sweet smell of sleep. Two of our three cats are only partly visible among the bedcovers; Rusty's whiskers sparkle in the sunlight. The old quilt, red appliqué on off-white, cuddles and cascades over the form of the one who gives this house so much meaning. The wide red border of the puff, with its tiny floral pattern, breaks into sun-splashed angles as if painted with a broad brush.

I laugh to myself as my eyes follow the Victorian contours of the old white iron bed with its brass knobs—the one I pulled from the dump, along with an old wicker rocker, rescuing these treasures by beating back flames with a beach towel.

"You crazy woman, you'll get burned!" David had yelled.

The beach is magnificent in the morning. The sand crunches beneath our feet and our breath is white before us. David and I so often start our day this way—the beach stretching ahead of us, the sun coming up over the harbor—a time to talk and share.

David often says that raising four teenagers is like trying to keep twenty-five Ping-Pong balls under water at the same time. One always keeps popping up. Kristen, who is doing so well at college, is now applying to the Sorbonne to spend her junior year abroad. Ronald, fascinated with photography and robotics, is looking at colleges with those interests in mind. Will the applications for the fall ever be completed? Then there's Jessica, prolifically reading and writing, soon to be a high school senior. I can't imagine only three of us around the dinner table!

Stephen seems happy to be home. David and I chuckled over the touching and humorous letter he sent this fall . . .

Mom and Dad,

There ain't nothing I can't take. I've felt better! But I'm growing up!

Oh, guess what? Doug and I were downstairs in the lav and I got there before he did, so I took his toilet paper. The officer of the day saw me so he dropped me [push-up position] in the middle of the bathroom and I knocked out 50! Doug laughed; my underpants weren't even all the way up and my nose had to touch the wet floor. There was urine on it. . . .

Our football team started out with 46 players, five went haywall (hopped the fence) and six are hurt. The coach says I'm a hacker. I'm on the punt team (v) and 2nd string cornerback (defensive back). The starters are the starting tailback, quarterback and another tailback. All are post grads or seniors.

Pop! We get up at 5:45 A.M., run two miles before first mess, and then go to first practice (for 2½ hours). That's before you probably get up. Ha ha! In practice we have six stations we go to. And all are hard as hell! When I go to them I just think that I'm "Hoāngbo" [Rambo] and nothing hurts. Pop! This place is murder! But I'm expendable here. It's like you hack it or you fall by the sidelines, and you become a quitter. And I'm not a quitter! Especially not in a sport like football!

The kids that went haywall are quitters. They fell by the wayside; two kids went last night, they were brothers. They jumped the wall after taps; they left all their stuff in their barracks. What wimps.

Mom, Pop, since I've been here I think I've grown up a lot! The coach has really brought out the man in me and the men in all of us. Well, football camp is almost over (in three days) and boot camp is gonna start . . . .

School starts tomorrow. Oh God! Say a prayer for me please! I can take the physical punishment but I can't (I don't think) take the school punishment.

I want you to know I pray for Ron, Jess, Kristen, and you, Mom and Dad. Dad, please say a prayer in church for the fullback that broke his leg in three places! I never know if it's gonna be me next. I pray God looks after our team and our coaches! God bless you all! Love 4 ever.

Mom, Dad, yesterday we were lined up in formation, out in the hall of the barracks. Three of us were told to re-rack (our chins weren't far back enough). In three counts you have to drop your head back, then forward, then pull in your chin. Mom, Dad, the three of us knocked ourselves out on the wall! When we got back on our feet, we were told, "Dummies, stand out from the wall a little next time. . . ." Everything went black!

———

"Mom?"

Stephen startles me; my daydreams and the sound of crackling bacon had masked his entrance.